The Gap Between

The Gap Between

LOVING and SUPPORTING
Someone with ALZHEIMER'S

Mary Moreland

BROWN BOOKS
PUBLISHING GROUP

Although this is not a work of fiction, the names of certain individuals referred to in the book have been changed in order to protect their privacy. Any similarity in name between a named person and anyone living or dead was not intended by the author and is purely coincidental.

This book is based on the personal experiences of the author. It is not intended to diagnose any condition and is not to be considered a substitute for consultation with a licensed professional. As the study of Alzheimer's is an evolving field in which methods, statistics, and terminology may change in response to new research, always consult your doctor before making any decisions regarding treatment.

The Gap Between
Loving and Supporting Someone with Alzheimer's

Brown Books Publishing Group
Dallas, TX / New York, NY
www.BrownBooks.com
(972) 381-0009

A New Era in Publishing®

Publisher's Cataloging-In-Publication Data

Names: Moreland, Mary, 1968- author.
Title: The gap between : loving and supporting someone with Alzheimer's / Mary
      Moreland.
Description: Dallas, TX ; New York, NY : Brown Books Publishing Group, [2022] |
      Includes bibliographical references.
Identifiers: ISBN 9781612545554 (hardcover)
Subjects: LCSH: Moreland, Mary, 1968---Family. | Caregivers--Biography. |
      Alzheimer's disease--Patients--Family relationships. | Alzheimer's disease--Patients-
      -Care. | Fathers--Death--Psychological aspects. | Loss (Psychology) | LCGFT:
      Autobiographies.
Classification: LCC RC523.2 .M67 2022 | DDC 362.1968310092--dc23

ISBN 978-1-61254-555-4
LCCN 2021922154

Printed in the United States
10 9 8 7 6 5 4 3 2 1

For more information or to contact the author, please go to
www.MaryMoreland.com.

To my sons,
for their unconditional support and encouragement.
You are both an inspiration to me.

CONTENTS

Poems by Jane P. Moreland

This is the book I wish I could have gifted to my younger self. Everyone's experience with Alzheimer's and caregiving is different. You may disagree with my point of view. Putting such raw and personal information into the public domain is difficult and makes me feel exposed. However, my purpose and hope in doing so is that there is a younger me out there who will find comfort and a friend through reading it.

I am not a medical professional. Rather, I am simply someone who, like so many others, has been touched by the disease of Alzheimer's. My mother lived with Alzheimer's for over a decade. As she was nearing the end of her journey, I felt immeasurable grief. Finding outlets for my grief was difficult, particularly in the age of COVID-19. I located a counselor on the internet who encouraged me to write my feelings in a journal.

What I discovered upon reading my journal was that I grieved not only the incremental loss of my mother, but also the loss of my status as caregiver. Being a member of the sandwich generation had become an important part of my identity.

Through writing and therapy, I discovered that I had not taken the time to process my loss and deal with my feelings. I did not nurture friendships. I brushed my sadness off to the side, thinking that I would deal with it later, because there were more important matters that needed my immediate attention. I learned that taking care of oneself, far from being indulgent, is necessary and important. Asking for help is not shameful.

I realized that there were things I could have done better in the care of my mother and of myself and that I should not feel guilty for those shortcomings. I tried my best. As I tell my children, if you genuinely try your best, you should feel proud. Revisiting and second-guessing is not helpful. Learning from an experience is valuable. Hopefully, there is something of value for you to learn in this book.

Acknowledgments

I would like to acknowledge and thank Dr. Ronald Holder PsyD, LPCS, who taught me the therapeutic benefit of writing and encouraged me to continue writing and to submit my manuscript for publication. I am a happier and more fulfilled person today no doubt because of his guidance.

I would like to thank my brothers. We always play as a team on the things that matter. I love you very much, and I thank you wholeheartedly for your support in including Mom's beautiful and thoughtful poetry in this book.

I am forever grateful for the many people who cared for my mother, particularly her primary care physician, our family caregivers, the personnel at her elder care facility, and her hospice provider. Mom continued to have a life even as the disease progressed. She was physically healthy, formed new friendships, and laughed, no doubt due to your wonderful care and support. Thank you for all you do.

I want to acknowledge the incredible resources available from the Alzheimer's Association, the Alzheimer's Society, the American Heart Association, the Family Caregiver Alliance, the National Institute on Aging, and AARP, which I have cited throughout the book. Thank you for your approval to cite these resources in this book.

I would like to acknowledge my wonderful mother, Jane Moreland. I will miss you always, but I am so happy for your poetry and short stories. I am still learning from you. I am excited to share your talent with others.

Finally, I would like to acknowledge and thank the team at Brown Books. They took a kernel and helped me to turn it into a book worthy of my mother.

Introduction

On June 2, 2012, I thought I knew what to expect from my mother's Alzheimer's diagnosis. I was a single mother of two young boys ages six and eight. An ambitious lawyer with goals and passion. A primary bread-winner. An optimist. A blonde-haired size four, comfortable in a bathing suit. I could handle anything thrown my way. Just watch me.

June 2, 2012: the day my father passed away unexpectedly. In some ways it was so long ago. I feel like a different person. I am more established and a bit wrinkly. I am now a mother of teenage sons, not young children. I am more private with fewer friends. Heavier with a menopausal belly. Fortunately, 2020 is a perfect cover—the COVID pandemic prevents one from being social (at least in person), and a "Zoom" top with yoga pants and sports shoes (or no shoes) meets all dress requirements.

In other ways, it could have happened only a minute ago. I can tap into those feelings and return to the scene. My mother's confused face after I asked her to call 911. The kind 911 operator who walked me through CPR while I yelled expletives into the phone and cried uncontrollably. I broke his rib. I know I did. I heard the crack and felt my hands push just a bit deeper into a new hollow in his chest. I can see the firemen storming into the bedroom with the energy of superheroes, only to quickly tell me it was too late. Of course, it was too late. He was dead before I arrived. I realize that now. Sometimes we see what we wish were true as if our will could create a parallel universe.

The day my father passed, my mother and I were going to the store to buy her a new cell phone. I called her before I left to pick her up. My parents referred to me as "Mare." "Oh, Mare, just pick something out.

1

You know what I like," my mother said. Completely understandable. I did know exactly what she liked. Personally, I dread buying a cell phone. So many choices. So many plans. I have no idea how much data I use. Just walking into the store raises my blood pressure and decreases my IQ score. "Besides, your father looks a bit ill. I think I should stay here in case he needs something."

"OK, I will pick out a phone and be right over." *Was he already dead?*

When I arrived, my mother said that Dad was taking a nap. We sat at the breakfast room table setting up her new phone. After I completed adding family members to her contacts, she asked if I would check on my father. "He didn't look well," she stated with a concerned tone. "I think there is something wrong with his cheek," she said while holding her hand next to her cheek.

I knew things were not right when I walked into the bedroom. I had never seen a dead body outside of a funeral home. My mind told me something was wrong, but I thought he was perhaps just very ill. After all, Dad had survived so many things. A quadruple bypass, back surgeries, high blood pressure, knee replacement, skin cancer, high cholesterol, and sleep apnea to name a few. A miracle of modern medicine. My mother asked me what I thought. "What should we do?"

I remember asking her slowly and in a calm voice to pick up the phone and call 911. When the operator joined, I heard her panicked voice tell the operator that she thought something was wrong with her husband, but she could not put the words together to explain or answer the questions. Trying not to sound upset, I asked her for the phone. She looked so confused and anguished. She looked helpless and sad. She looked scared and vulnerable. My heart broke, but I needed to attend to more immediate matters. I had to block her out of my mind and talk to the operator.

As I described the scene, my brain realized the full effect of the moment. The operator asked me if I knew CPR. I said no. She asked me if I had taken a CPR class. I told her that I had taken a CPR class at work, but that I had never used it. I recall that she told me not to worry and just to listen and do as she said. This is when the tears started streaming through the wrinkles around my eyes, like creeks from melting snow down my cheeks. "Dad, no, shit, fuck, no, no, no, come on, Dad!" She calmly walked me through CPR, although it sounded like she also was crying. Like muscle memory it came back. I was surprised that the feeling of pressing down on the chest of the mannequin during my CPR class at work and the feeling of pressing down on the chest of my father were, in my mind, the same. I recall feeling a sense of calm and accomplishment when I felt the chest reduce when I applied my weight and return once I reduced my pressure. I put my full weight into it—if we are going to perform CPR, let's put everything into it.

The doctor was called. The police arrived. The police attempted to interview my mother until I realized what was happening and intervened.

Yes, she used to put his daily heart medication in his pill container. No, they had a happy marriage. More than fifty years. No, she would not have intentionally made a mistake—she seems a bit confused. Please, talk to me. Please, do not ask her any more questions. She is upset, confused, vulnerable. Let me tell you about her Alzheimer's. She was diagnosed several months ago. Please just let her be. She is very confused, I agree. You are right.

Close relatives I had called to inform about my father's passing ate sandwiches in the breakfast room from groceries my mother had purchased. Horrible phone calls etched in my brain—sons learning of their father's passing. I did not know that almost a decade later I would make the same phone calls about my mother.

My father lay dead in his bed waiting for the hearse to take him away. The police stayed until the hearse arrived. Although they were not supposed to allow me to sit with him, I felt an overwhelming need to be next to him. They kindly obliged. I sat next to his body and wondered if it were just a shell. I prayed. I wished for a sign. *Where is his soul, his essence? Is it just over? Is this how it ends? Does something happen afterward?* I thought perhaps I would receive a sign, something showing me what happens after our bodies wear out. I finally summoned the fortitude to touch his shoulder. It was cold and stiff. No one was home.

A representative of the funeral home eventually arrived that evening in a dark suit and entered the house carrying a single long-stemmed red rose that he presented to my mother with his condolences. She broke out in fits of giggles and laughter. He shot a confused look at my teary face.

If only I had realized . . . these were the good times.

I have since learned more about death, and I know that my father had what people call a good death. He enjoyed a lunch with his friends at a favorite restaurant. He came home and talked to his wife of fifty years. Later I learned from my mother that he had kissed her on the cheek and told her to place his wallet and watch in her purse. He went upstairs to take an afternoon nap and changed into the navy blue, silky pajamas that he loved. He died in his sleep.

THE PROGRESS OF GRIEF

By Jane P. Moreland

Grief is at first private, fallen acorns
held tightly within lacquered shells,
stone-hard pears and pomegranates
   that cannot release sweet tears.

   It becomes the somber pigeon
released every dawn and home by dusk
to find you in umber shade of live oak,
   follow your escape through scars
into the private hollow that could split
   like your heart, spill tears like rain
   to run widening through shallows
   and remembered crevices, abrade
   your inner landscape, wash you
in cold currents over deep floors and out
into sunlight, where you find yourself
crossing fields on a murky fast canal
   that is the bold stroke across canvas
that severs then from now, life as absolute
   before the blurry gold becoming.

Chapter 1

Facts about Alzheimer's Disease

Alzheimer's disease undoubtedly carries a social stigma. So often when family or friends learn of an Alzheimer's diagnosis, they presume their loved one is suddenly incapable of making decisions, enjoying life, or contributing to society. There is a feeling that all is lost. I reluctantly admit that, upon learning of my mother's diagnosis, I felt several of these emotions. The worst-case scenario had occurred—Alzheimer's disease.

I accompanied my mother on her Alzheimer's journey for over a decade. Reflecting upon that experience, I now appreciate that, just like how coronary artery disease is a type of heart disease, Alzheimer's disease is simply a type of brain disease. It is a progressive disease, meaning that symptoms gradually worsen over several years, and individuals eventually lose the ability to understand and react to their environment.[1] We do not marginalize, isolate, or exclude people living with coronary heart disease; we should not do so to people living with Alzheimer's disease. Learning about the disease and correcting misinformation will break the Alzheimer's stigma.

Alzheimer's is an irreversible brain disease that is ultimately fatal. An individual with Alzheimer's does not detect or notice initial changes to the brain. These initial changes begin twenty years or more before symptoms begin. Examples of Alzheimer's symptoms are memory loss and difficulty doing routine tasks. Symptoms are caused by damage to nerve cells in parts of the brain involved with cognitive function—i.e., memory, learning, and thinking. As the disease continues to develop, nerve cells in other parts of the brain are also affected. At the late stage of the disease, the nerve cells in the brain are so damaged that the person living with Alzheimer's is unable to walk, swallow, and carry out other basic bodily functions. Individuals with late-stage Alzheimer's eventually require twenty-four-hour care and are bedridden.[2]

Dementia can come in many forms; Alzheimer's is the most common type.[3] Alzheimer's is the sixth-leading cause of death in the United States[4] and kills more people than breast cancer and prostate cancer combined.[5] Alzheimer's dementia is much more prevalent than one may think. In fact, over 11 percent of people 65 and older live with this disease. Unless there are developments or medical breakthroughs to prevent, slow, or cure Alzheimer's disease, the number of people age 65 and older with Alzheimer's in the United States may grow to nearly 13 million.[6]

Alzheimer's disease is a global problem. According to the World Health Organization, currently more than 55 million people live with dementia worldwide, and there are nearly 10 million new cases every year. Alzheimer's disease may contribute to 60–70 percent of such cases.[7] The number of people affected is set to rise to 139 million by 2050, with the greatest increases in low- and middle-income countries. A new case of dementia arises somewhere in the world every 3 seconds.[8]

The Alzheimer's Disease Continuum

The Alzheimer's disease continuum (shown below) illustrates the progression of brain changes a person living with Alzheimer's undergoes. Initially, these changes, which take place deep inside one's brain, are unnoticeable to the person affected. However, these brain changes eventually cause problems with memory and ultimately result in physical disability.

The continuum consists of three broad phases: (1) preclinical Alzheimer's disease; (2) mild cognitive impairment; and (3) dementia (see Figure 1). Within the third phase are three additional phases—mild, moderate, and severe. These three sub-phases reflect at what degree symptoms interfere with one's ability to carry out everyday activities.[9]

Alzheimer's Disease (AD) Continuum*

Preclinical AD	Mild Cognitive Impairment due to AD	Dementia due to AD Mild	Dementia due to AD Moderate	Dementia due to AD Severe
No symptoms	Very mild symptoms that do not interfere with everyday activities	Symptoms interfere with some everyday activities	Symptoms interfere with many everyday activities	Symptoms interfere with most everyday activities

*Although these arrows are of equal size, the components of the AD continuum are not equal in duration.

Figure 1. Alzheimer's Disease (AD) Continuum chart.[10]

The length of time an individual spends in each phase of the continuum varies from person to person. A number of factors—such as sex, age, and genetics—influence the time period of each phase. Although a person with Alzheimer's lives an average of four to eight years after diagnosis, it is possible for an individual to live as long as twenty years after diagnosis.[11]

Preclinical Alzheimer's Disease

Changes in the brain related to Alzheimer's begin years before any outward signs of the disease noticed by you or those around you. During preclinical Alzheimer's disease, the brain compensates for these changes, enabling the individual to function normally. Stated differently, although a person has measurable brain changes indicating early signs of Alzheimer's disease, this person does not yet experience memory loss or even know his or her brain is changing. [12]

Mild Cognitive Impairment (MCI) due to Alzheimer's Disease

During MCI, the brain can no longer compensate for the damage to nerve cells caused by Alzheimer's disease. Therefore, in addition to evidence of brain changes, people with MCI also experience slight cognitive problems, such as complications with memory and thinking. The individual, family members, and friends may notice these subtle changes. Because these cognitive problems do not interfere with performing everyday activities, memory lapses or problems in thinking may not be noticeable to others who do not know your loved one well.[13]

Dementia due to Alzheimer's Disease

During the third phase of the disease, the evidence of Alzheimer's-related brain changes is now accompanied by noticeable cognitive changes that impair a person's ability to carry out everyday activities.[14] The individual has difficulty functioning in daily life due to symptoms such as memory lapses and confusion. The date at which an individual crosses from MCI to Alzheimer's dementia is usually impossible to identify.[15] As the dementia phase of Alzheimer's progresses from mild to moderate to severe, it is common for individuals to experience many different types of symptoms that can change over time, which is a reflection of the degree of damage in different parts of the brain.[16]

The speed of progression from mild to moderate to severe Alzheimer's dementia differs from person to person. Since Alzheimer's disease affects people in different ways, each person may experience symptoms differently. It also may be difficult to place a person with Alzheimer's in a specific stage as stages may overlap.[17] To make matters even more complicated, someone living with Alzheimer's may pass very slowly through one stage, but much more quickly through another, which is something I personally experienced with my mother.

Early-Stage Alzheimer's Dementia (Mild)

In the early stage of Alzheimer's, a person may function independently. He or she may still drive, work, and be part of social activities. Despite this, the person may feel as if he or she is having memory lapses, such as forgetting familiar words or the location of everyday objects.[18]

Symptoms may not be widely apparent at this stage, but family and close friends may take notice, and a doctor would be able to identify symptoms using certain diagnostic tools. Symptoms might be put down to other causes such as stress or depression or generally getting older. [19]

Common difficulties include the following:

- Coming up with the right word or name
- Remembering names when introduced to new people
- Having difficulty performing tasks in social or work settings

- Forgetting material that was just read
- Losing or misplacing a valuable object
- Experiencing increased trouble with planning or organizing[20]

Middle-Stage Alzheimer's Dementia (Moderate)

Middle-stage Alzheimer's is typically the longest stage and can last for many years. As the disease progresses, the person with Alzheimer's will require a greater level of care.[21]

During the middle stage of Alzheimer's, the dementia symptoms are more pronounced. The person may confuse words, get frustrated or angry, and act in unexpected ways, such as refusing to bathe. Damage to nerve cells in the brain can also make it difficult for the person to express thoughts and perform routine tasks without assistance.[22]

Symptoms, which vary from person to person, may include these:

- Being forgetful of events or personal history
- Feeling moody or withdrawn, especially in socially or mentally challenging situations
- Being unable to recall information about themselves, like their address or telephone number and the high school or college they attended
- Experiencing confusion about where they are or what day it is
- Requiring help choosing proper clothing for the season or the occasion
- Having trouble controlling their bladder and bowels
- Experiencing changes in sleep patterns, such as sleeping during the day and becoming restless at night
- Showing an increased tendency to wander and become lost
- Demonstrating personality and behavioral changes, including suspiciousness and delusions or compulsive, repetitive behavior, like hand-wringing or tissue shredding[23]

In the middle stage, the person living with Alzheimer's can still participate in daily activities with assistance. It's important to find out what the person can still do or find ways to simplify tasks. As the need for more intensive care increases, caregivers may want to consider respite care or an adult day care center so they can have a temporary break from caregiving while the person living with Alzheimer's continues to receive care in a safe environment.[24]

Late-Stage Alzheimer's Dementia (Severe)

In the final stage of the disease, dementia symptoms are severe. Individuals lose the ability to respond to their environment, to carry on a conversation and, eventually, to control movement. They may still say words or phrases, but communicating pain becomes difficult. As memory and cognitive skills continue to worsen, significant personality changes may take place, and individuals need extensive care.[25]

At this stage, individuals may experience the following:

- Requiring around-the-clock assistance with daily personal care
- Losing awareness of recent experiences as well as of their surroundings
- Experiencing changes in physical abilities, including walking, sitting, and, eventually, swallowing
- Having difficulty communicating
- Becoming vulnerable to infections, especially pneumonia[26]

The person living with Alzheimer's may not be able to initiate engagement as much during the late stage, but he or she can still benefit from interaction in ways that are appropriate, like listening to relaxing music or receiving reassurance through gentle touch. During this stage, caregivers may want to use support services, such as hospice care, which focus on providing comfort and dignity at the end of life.[27] Hospice can be of great benefit to people—and their families—who are in the final stages of Alzheimer's and other dementias.

BEQUEST

By Jane P. Moreland

Begin afterlife, treadle machine with curliqued grilles,
complacent with black oak drawers full of tissue patterns,
cushions of needles, silk elastic, eyelet lace,
varicolored threads and buttons, bobbins, thimbles, shears,
cubbyholes of snaps, zippers, chalks.

You could tell of chambray smocks and pinafores,
gossamer skirts with whalebone hoops, three satin wedding gowns,
of crepe de Chine and Christmas velvet,
moiré taffeta, tulle, voile, chintz,
how the two of you, humming, stitched love into dreams.

Understand: I do not hum,
but swear, rip more than stitch.
I sew no gowns,
but seams of seats, knee patches in breeches,
and only under threat of nakedness.

Chapter 2

Diagnosis and Understanding

June 2, 2012.

So much more than a hot Houston summer day. The day my father died. The day I joined the sandwich generation.

The day my third child, Jane, was born.

Jane was an unusual child. A Benjamin Button child. Born as a teenager, she aged into a baby. Unlike my sons who accomplished new challenges and depth of thought as they grew, Jane slowly lost her abilities. An accomplished writer and gracious Southern woman, she wore "female underwear," needed a lift to get in and out of bed, and was unable to dress herself at the end of her life. Still, I adored my Jane from the time she was my mother, through her teenage years, elementary school, and day care. She was always my mother. Her hands were always the same elegant hands. I loved her when she recognized me and when she did not. When she was a baby, I lovingly stroked Baby Jane's face, stared into her eyes, and told her how special and loved she was, just as I had done with my children.

After my father's death, friends stopped by to see my mother and pay their respects. Sometimes they unknowingly sat in my father's chair. At the time, it was shocking. In retrospect, of course they did. It was a chair. Just a chair, not My Father's Sacred Chair. My mother would sit in her usual place on the couch, I occupied the salmon-colored chair, and the family friend relaxed unknowingly in Dad's chair.

"He was a great man and friend. I am so sorry, Jane."

"I'm sorry. Excuse me . . . Who was your friend?"

It went downhill from there.

Odd sideways glances from old family friends. Confused looks transmitted my way. I waited for the phone call after each visit, apologizing for the message about to be delivered, but gently telling me that I might consider a doctor's appointment for my mother as soon as possible. Most never returned or called again. At the time this annoyed me greatly. Lifelong friends until one is ill. However, now that I am a bit wrinkly, I understand. I also realize that I never asked any of these friends for help or support. *Were they waiting for me to reach out to them? Did they assume that I would ask if I needed help?* Friends with direct dementia experience were invaluable, inspirational, and full of helpful advice.

My mother had been formally diagnosed in the fall of 2011. My father called me at work and informed me of the diagnosis. Alzheimer's was our big secret. Do not tell anyone. This is Family Information. Not for public consumption. Thinking back, while I realize this was an effort to protect my mother, it should not have been a secret. There was nothing to be ashamed of. Alzheimer's is an illness, just like cancer or coronary heart disease are illnesses. Rather than hiding Mom and staying at home so that she would not be placed in what I assumed would be awkward situations or crying over things she no longer could do, I should have celebrated all the things she still could do—we should have taken day trips to the Texas hill country to see the bluebonnets and visited her sister more often at the beach. *Did we deprive her many friends' ability to tell her goodbye? Would informing her friends have brought her comfort? Did our efforts to protect her result in her feeling alone?*

June 2, 2012. I never planned for this day. My father was the man who had survived health scare after health scare, always winning. He was my rock. My teacher and adviser. He loved me unconditionally even when I annoyed him. When I saw him prior to the attempts at CPR, he was in his bed with his hands gripping his sheet and blanket, pulling it upward like he was covering himself. When I spoke with his doctor, the doctor told me that he went to bed and never woke up. In his mind he is still taking a long nap. I am thankful for this good death but wished he had called 911 rather than giving Mom his wallet and watch. Selfishly, I would have liked to spend a bit more time with him.

Did he give her his wallet and watch? Is that what happened? We will never know. *How else would the watch and wallet make it into her purse?* She told me that Dad announced he was going to take a nap, got up from his chair in the living room, walked over to her on her usual place on the couch, gave her a kiss on the cheek, and told her to put his wallet and watch in her purse. His watch was a gift from her. Her watch was a gift from him (and identical to mine). Both watches had engraved notes to each other on the back, as does mine.

We discovered this when talking to my mother several days after his death when she produced the wallet and watch from her purse and said we might need them. "I have his watch and wallet," she said out of the blue and removed them from her black leather purse. She recounted the events of that day. She told us that he said she would need these things and watched her as she placed the wallet and watch into her handbag and zipped the handbag shut. *What else occurred? What else did he say? Did he say anything about his children or grandchildren, or did he just tell her he loved her? Did he know he was going to die, or did he just feel ill? Did he see a sign?* Was my mother's recollection correct? We will never know. However, he always placed his watch and wallet in the same location next to his chair, which most certainly was not in my mother's purse.

Shortly after my father died, I took my mother to a grief meeting at the church. We sat in a circle while each person spoke of his or her grief. When it was my mother's time to speak, she said her husband had recently passed. She then told the story of how they met. An adorable anecdote about a sophomore at college living in the sorority house on phone duty. She ran tirelessly up and down the stairs each time the phone rang, fetching the lucky sorority sister to come and talk to her gentleman suitor. She was dating someone, but then a handsome young man came to the door for his date with another sister. Her heart stopped. The rest is history.

All I could do was cry. My parents did not attend the same college. They met in their early twenties when they both lived in Houston and were both working. She was a chemist at the time. I believe it was a blind date. The circle thought I was crying over the death of my father. I was not.

On the way home, Mom asked me where my father was. I explained (again).

A few days later, she told me my father had left her for another woman. She did not understand why. She thinks he met her during a business trip to New York. I explained (again). *Will he come back? Why did he leave? Where is he? What happened to him, Mare?*

My parents had celebrated their fiftieth wedding anniversary a year prior. My father insisted on a party. He gave a beautiful toast. His eyes teared, and his voice wavered. People who attended assumed it was due to a man who had loved his wife and mother of his children for fifty years. The few of us with the Family Information knew it was also because that woman was slowly leaving us—and by the time we noticed and were able to accept and confront it, had already left us in many ways. There was no "goodbye." No "I love you." I never told her how much I admired and respected her. Apart from the casual "love you," I never told her how I felt. I would tell her later, but at that time it would be more for me than for her. Telling Baby Jane just wasn't the same as telling Mom. I watched my mother during the toast. It was like she was hearing the story for the first time. I guess we were all a bit teary.

There was a time during Mom's progression when I thought I could get her back. I could spend time talking to her, reminding her of points in her life, and eventually she would have a moment of lucidity. It was an emotional journey. It took time. When we arrived at the point she seemed to remember, I was exhausted, but hopeful. I thought if we continued this exercise regularly, perhaps she would snap back. I now wonder if she remembered. *Did she return to lucidity or just figure out what to say to make me stop asking so many questions?* I will always believe she returned because thinking otherwise is just too painful.

I have spent a lot of time wondering why I did not notice the slow deterioration. I lived only a mile away—bicycle distance. I saw my parents frequently. Other relatives who visited less frequently noticed things I did not. My parents and I would talk about the audacity of comments made by other family members regarding Mom's mental state. We were collectively offended. The allegations were shocking. When small incidents of forgetfulness occurred, we agreed not to inform other family members, because they would "overreact" and "blow things out of proportion." Mom always agreed. *Was she just agreeing with us to avoid admitting something was wrong? Did she think anything was wrong?*

In retrospect, I think it's easier not to notice a bit-by-bit deterioration in someone's ability than to notice a change over time. I now see the past with a new perspective. My mother used to enjoy driving—or maybe she had simply been traumatized by teaching her teenager children how to drive and wanted to be in control of the car. Either way, she always drove when we went on an errand, shopping, or out to lunch. At some point, I started driving. "Would you like to drive?" she would ask. I never really minded driving, so I would always say yes. I did not think anything odd about it, except that I was flattered she asked. *Has she finally decided I'm a good driver?* I thought. In retrospect I wonder, *Did she not want to drive? Was she worried about her driving?*

A few times my father called me looking for my mother. "Is she at your house? I haven't seen her for hours." When Mom returned, she would explain that things just took longer, and she decided to run a few additional errands. *Honestly, who has not done that?* Maybe she just wanted to be alone for a while. Maybe she went to a museum. Perhaps she was working on a short story. Maybe she visited someone. Maybe she went clothes shopping. Now I wonder if she had gotten lost. *Was she confused, and that's why things took a long time? Did she lose track of time?*

My mother always enjoyed clothing. She was one of the most elegant and classy women I have known. She had a reasonably sized and very well-organized walk-in closet. Now that I reflect on her life, I realize that a couple of years before her diagnosis she began hanging a small quantity of clothing on the outside of her closet and selecting her daily wardrobe from those clothes. She "organized" her sweaters in her office so that she could see which ones still fit, but most never made their way back into drawers. *Had the choice of clothing in the closet become overwhelming? Were items never returned to drawers purposefully? Was this simplification and putting things out in the open due to her Alzheimer's?*

My mother used to prepare elaborate meals for the family when everyone was in town together, typically during the holidays. She took pride in a well-set table. Although attire was casual, the affair was formal with place cards, a thoughtful centerpiece, silver goblets, and wedding China. At some point there were no place cards. She said that she decided to embrace the informality of the age. There is truth in that statement, and my mother was always changing, becoming more modern. *However, was it really that she did not remember the names of everyone who would attend?* Around the same time, there were too few seats set at the table. *Could she no longer equate the number of people to seats required?* Holiday gifts were misplaced. Christmas stockings for certain people were missing. Typically, visitors came for holidays—always a lot to do. I attributed these things to the excitement of company and the stress of wanting everything to be just right.

When cleaning out my father's office, I found a copy of a thank-you letter to a restaurant praising an employee. Apparently, my mother lost her wallet at a party at the restaurant. The employee located and returned the wallet to my parents at their home (the address of which was on my mother's driver's license) on his own accord. When offered a reward, he declined. According to the letter, the wallet must have fallen out of her purse.

One day I visited my mother, and there was a very ugly plastic table-cloth covering an old folding card table in the middle of the kitchen. "A Kitchen Island," she said. To see if she liked having a kitchen island. It was also easier for Dad to find his snacks. He would no longer need to ask her where they were and could help himself. Self-service at last! We should all be more self-sufficient, she insisted. She even put favorite snacks for my kids on the new island. Ugly, yet functional. A test of the island. No need to commit if we don't like it. As a mother of two small children, I appreciated the idea of a self-service island. Looking back now, I wonder, *Did she want everything out in the open and used the island as an excuse? How could someone be confused but simultaneously so clever?*

Preparing for the Journey of Alzheimer's

Take observations from friends and relatives seriously.
If you see your loved one often, you may not notice the deterioration as much as someone who visits less frequently. I visited my mother regularly, but it was unusual for us to spend more than a few hours together at a time. She always had logical explanations for items that, in retrospect, were clearly signs of her Alzheimer's. I accepted these explanations at face value. Out-of-town relatives who visited less frequently, but for longer stretches of time, realized something was terribly wrong. Now, I know we should have taken their comments seriously.

Don't fall for the Alzheimer's stigma.
Individuals living with Alzheimer's can continue to contribute to society, be social, and have fun. Although you will need to adjust activities as the disease progresses, don't fall for the stigma that your loved one can't make decisions or is no longer present because of an Alzheimer's diagnosis. My mother continued to write short stories, enjoy my children's school events, exercise regularly, and arrange flowers well after her diagnosis. As the disease progressed, we simplified our activities, but continued to have fun together. After she moved to an assisted living facility, she made new friends, participated in field trips, and thoroughly enjoyed her classes. She continued classes when she lived on the memory care floor. She sang songs, loved listening to music at the facility's weekly concerts, and participated in activities. She indulged her sweet tooth. Even during her

final hours, she enjoyed listening to piano music. Although you will need to meet your loved one where he or she is in the Alzheimer's journey, you can still enjoy each other. In retrospect, I wish I had focused more on what remained rather than mourning what did not. During the early and middle stages of the disease, I avoided certain activities because I assumed she would feel uncomfortable or awkward. On reflection, I wish I had discussed my concerns with her, rather than presumed I knew what was best.

When life changes unexpectedly, have compassion for yourself.
An unexpected moment on an ordinary Saturday afternoon can mark the "before" and "after" of your life. This is an important milestone many of us face. Even though you know your loved one is in ill health or getting older, that person's death can still be shocking and form a permanent marker in your life that will forever remind you of the before and after. Have compassion for yourself. This is a new experience. You do not need to know everything at once. There are typically many steps that must be taken after someone passes, such as informing friends and relatives, funeral arrangements, legal matters, closing accounts, and dealing with personal possessions. This can be overwhelming both emotionally and mentally. However, most of these things do not need to be done immediately. Focus on what must be done in the moment.

Grief is a process that takes time. You do not need to feel alone.
Don't expect to bounce back quickly. Let the grief wash over you. Journal. Connect with other people. Talk to friends, a counselor, or people at your place of worship. If you are alone, look for a grief counseling group, volunteer chaplains, or other bereavement counselors who can offer support. Available resources to locate such groups or persons are hospice organizations, churches and places of worship, funeral homes, hospitals, online resources, and wellness centers. Seek out people who have lived through a similar experience. Call the Alzheimer's Association or read their online literature.

If you do not prefer group settings, books about Alzheimer's disease and grief can be valuable tools. There are also a number of excellent podcasts and radio shows about Alzheimer's and dementia. Download an episode and listen to it during a walk or your commute to work. Lori La Bey's Alzheimer's Speaks Radio and the Alzheimer's Speaks website are a treasure trove of friendship, advice, and resources. Another wonderful, engaging, and uplifting podcast is Love Conquers Alz, whose host created an Oscar-qualified short film about her mother's Alzheimer's, named *My Mom and the Girl*, a film definitely worth twenty minutes of your time. The Alzheimer's Association Helpline is a free, twenty-four-hour resource for questions about the disease, emotional support, and care. You do not need to feel alone.

Empower yourself by learning CPR.

Cardiopulmonary resuscitation (CPR) is a procedure that is performed when the heart stops beating to maintain an active blood flow in the body. CPR extends the opportunity for trained medical personnel to successfully resuscitate an individual.[1] Emergencies can happen anywhere and at any time. According to the American Heart Association, over 88 percent of heart attacks occur in the home.[2] Therefore, the life you save with CPR is most likely to be someone you love: a child, a spouse, a parent, or a friend. Knowing CPR can give you confidence in an emergency. However, for many people attempting CPR, it is a frightening and intimidating experience, and you may feel conflicted about pressing down so hard on your loved one's chest. You may feel like you are hurting your loved one. On the contrary, according to the American Heart Association, "your actions can only help."[3] Don't be afraid. Even if your efforts at CPR are futile, knowing that you tried something in a moment of crisis can bring great peace. CPR classes are readily available. You can locate a class through the American Red Cross, the American Heart Association, the YMCA, and local hospitals and universities, among other locations. Classes are relatively short; you can empower yourself and protect your loved ones and community by learning how to save a life in a few short hours.

If you upset your loved one in the name of safety, don't feel guilty.

A person living with Alzheimer's is an adult and deserves to be treated like one; however, sometimes—such as for safety reasons or to deal with an immediate matter—the caregiver must step in like a parent in a loving and respectful manner. Like you might do with a toddler, a caregiver may need to remove a potentially dangerous object from the individual's hand or move the individual to a safe location while tending to a more pressing matter. This may upset the person living with Alzheimer's and cause anguish, discomfort, or even anger. The strategies you might use with a child—explaining why, reasoning, repeating something the child did not hear—will not work with someone living with Alzheimer's. Do not feel guilty, but do try to maintain a respectful tone and speak to your loved one in a polite and loving manner.

Tell people how to help you.

Accept help when offered, and don't be embarrassed to ask for help. You do not need to feel alone. Keep in mind that people may very much want to help you, but they don't know how. This makes sense, because these people may not have experience with Alzheimer's or other forms of dementia. Therefore, you may need to tell them how to help you, for example: *Could you watch my kids for the afternoon while I take a break? Could you go pick up some things at the store for me? Could you pick up my children from school every Monday so that I could go to a support group or run some errands?* The worst scenario is for you to feel alone thinking no one wants to help you, while others desperately want to assist but just do not know how.

A Visit

By Jane P. Moreland

She comes in with a box
of blue iris and white penstemon,
wires and shears: the tools of control.

She tours my house,
noticing dracaenas, angel wing begonias
in terra cotta pots, soil visible,
root hairs exposed at old fissures,
doesn't miss ivy, russet coleus
rooting in muddy crystal bowls.
I know her silence:
thick smoke of disapproval.

She cheers the hall arrangement,
three shades of red poppies in a blue vase,
I put there half to mock her.

She calls me to the kitchen
as she arches stems to widths and heights
defined by a porcelain urn.
I watch in silence my mother working
at our shared obsession, thinking how
in the gap between us,
someone could plant sequoias.

Chapter 3

Communicating with Your Loved One

It is tempting to just agree with someone with dementia. When they say something that's incorrect or makes no sense, it is easy to agree with whatever they say. It is the less painful choice. It is also the faster choice. I am guilty of having made that choice from time to time. However, at least with my mother, particularly at the beginning of her disease, correcting her was the better and more respectful choice on most topics.

Lovingly correct your loved one. Bring them into the moment. Kindly tell them that it is not Wednesday, but Monday, while referring to a clock or calendar. That you are not their mother, but their child, while showing them a family photo. That you do not think they need to buy more milk because we just bought some earlier today, and kindly show them the recently purchased milk. Be patient and ask questions to try to really understand what they need. If these strategies do not work, you can try to distract the person by talking about something else or moving to a different room. Every dynamic and person is different. What works for one person may not work for another.

My mother frequently asked about my father's whereabouts after his passing. She created scenarios in her mind of what had transpired, such as my father leaving her for another woman. She had completely forgotten the events of June 2 and his subsequent funeral. Initially, I explained that he had passed on. However, when she was lucid enough to understand this explanation, the surprising news of her husband's demise was devastating. She experienced this death repeatedly with each explanation. Eventually, I began telling her that he was in a safe place and loved her very much. Then, I would change the topic. This was the kinder, more loving choice, even though it was not 100 percent truthful.

There were several boxes in the garage filled with old items. Unexpectedly, and despite my assurances to the contrary, my mother decided that I was kicking her out of her house. She was on the cusp of homelessness. These boxes contained my things that I planned to move into my new home with my children after I dumped my mother on the streets of Houston. She would sneak into the garage to look at the boxes. She informed others of my evil plan. "How could Mare do this to me?" My brother cleverly labeled the boxes "Jane's Belongings," "Property of Jane," and "Belongs to Jane" in bold black sharpie marker. A simple trick that worked. Evil plan forgotten.

Despite my children's young ages at the beginning of Mom's disease, their empathy and patience floored me. I recall one day when my mother came over for lunch. While I was cooking in the kitchen, she asked my younger son no less than twenty times, "What grade are you in?" Each time he kindly and respectfully replied with his grade and the name of his school, only to be asked again after a few minutes. After she left, he said to me, "Well, I bet there is one question you don't want to ask me," and walked down the hall to his room.

Mom used to call me at around five in the morning and ask me what happened to her children. "I just need to know what happened to them," she would state. I told her that she was in luck because I was Mary. She was always very happy to have located Mary. "Oh, Mare! I am so happy it's you!" I would give her an overview of my brothers' lives. Where they lived. How many children they each had. How they were very happy. How they both loved her so much. How her grandchildren loved their Grandma Jane. Relieved, she would thank me and hang up, only to call again a few minutes later with the same initial questions. After three or four times, she would stop calling. At the time, I remember thinking, *Be happy for this.* Your mother knows who you are and can call you. Simultaneously, I was annoyed and just very tired. I never understood why she stopped calling, but I was glad she did. I needed to get breakfast and get dressed and ready for school and work.

Such conflicting emotions. Of course, I wanted to go to her house. I was sad and just wanted to be with her. Give her a hug. Call my siblings together. Let her hear their voices. I was also extremely worried. But, as a single parent, my children needed their routine and to get to school on time. They deserved a fully engaged mother. They deserved a good breakfast. Getting them ready took time and effort. Getting myself ready for work took time as well. All you can do is your best.

People living with Alzheimer's lose their filter. Sometimes this is disturbing, and sometimes it is funny, at least momentarily. Sometimes, it is just sad. When it is momentarily funny, it eventually turns to sadness once you reflect and think later. It's a laugh in the moment, but sometimes a laugh in the moment is what you need.

A friend of ours had gained quite a bit of weight. My mother had a beautiful figure. She worked at it. Weights, sit-ups, salads, stationary bicycle. She was quite critical of overweight people. Once she drove to my house with a pile of her "fat pants" after cleaning out her closet. The family friend rang the doorbell at my parents' house. My mother opened the door, looked at this person's stomach, looked at her face, and said, "oink, oink."

"What did your mom say, Mary?" I was asked. I replied, "Oh, she said it's nice to see you." My mother looked at me, rolled her eyes in disgust, and walked away.

Her doctor told me it was like she no longer had a "save as" button on the computer. The hard drive was full. Nothing could be added. What was on the drive would slowly decay—maybe the oldest things on the drive would decay last. At the time it made sense, but in retrospect, it does not. Or maybe the hard drive had just been wiped clean much earlier than I realized, and the social graces and intelligence of my mother allowed us not to see it.

Several years later, when I cleaned out her home, I found sticky notes over sticky notes. My phone number on a sticky note by each phone.

Reminders. Notes. Walls of sticky notes. Assorted colors of sticky notes. Things out in the open. Items that should be in drawers moved to countertops for all to see.

When did she know? She must have known. Did she know? Was she in denial? How did she feel? If she knew, why didn't she tell me? Did she think I could not handle it? Did she think it would go away? Did she purposely not tell anyone, thinking, eventually, it would not matter? Did she try to tell me, but I was too absorbed in my busy life?

The last eight and a half years of my life are a blur. I have done many things, this is true. My children have grown. I was there for all of it, but none of it. Perhaps all parents feel this way. Time passes slowly, until it does not.

I remember a day when my child left the car for school with his shirt on backwards. That was the best I could do on that day. "Your shirt is on backward!" exclaimed the teacher at the carpool. "Really?!" I said. "Oh, my goodness! Oh dear, I am sorry!" I knew the shirt was backward; it was just all I could do to arrive on time, in clothing, after breakfast, with teeth brushed and a backpack. *After all, he did have a shirt on, right?* Just needed a little tweaking, but the fundamentals were there! The shirt was backward, but we arrived on time at school with a shirt—on his body. Arriving to school on time meant that I would arrive to work on time. The backward shirt was a simple fix through a trip to the bathroom. Writing this now, I wonder how I did not have the time, energy, or desire to fix my son's shirt, but at the time, just getting to school was all I could manage.

Where did the time go? I was so busy. But at the same time, life was slow. So many things have happened in the last decade: I have had two knee surgeries—one an entire knee replacement—my children have hit milestone after milestone, we have new pets, Obama was president for eight years, Donald Trump was president, there is a global pandemic. Normally, I would have discussed these things with my mother—she was alive for all of it, but cognizant of none.

There were so many times I longed for my mother. Before I had my knee replacement, I remembered how she had come to Virginia when I had my tonsils out to take care of me. When I got a promotion, I wanted to tell her about it and hear her say she was proud of me. When my kids reached milestones, I wanted her to be a part of it. I still told her about these things, but she could not comprehend them. It wasn't her fault. It was the disease's fault.

Each time I visited my mother I allowed myself to cry on the way to my car. Once I arrived at the car, the crying must stop. Later, the rule changed, such that I could cry to the car, in the car, but once in front of my house, the crying must stop. Then the rule changed such that it was okay to cry until I entered the house. Later, I could not cry again until I entered my room. What crazy rules. I should have just cried whenever, wherever I wanted! That would have been a lot healthier.

Tips for Effective Communication

Fewer choices are better.

Providing a choice to someone living with Alzheimer's is empowering, but too many choices are overwhelming. This is because your loved one cannot process information as he or she used to do in the past. Overstimulation can cause anger, frustration, or anxiety. Provide your loved one a choice with two options. *Would you like A or B? Would you like water or orange juice? Would you like to wear the red shirt or the blue shirt today?*

Consider a kitchen (or other) inventory list to avoid unnecessary purchases.

A kitchen inventory for food is helpful so that the same items are not purchased repeatedly. Your loved one will not realize they have purchased the same items over and over. Not even a mustard enthusiast needs eight containers of mustard. At the early stage of the disease, having an inventory will allow you to show your loved one why certain purchases are not necessary and will avoid spending money on items that will not be used.

Tips for dealing with paranoia:

Some people living with Alzheimer's experience periods of paranoia. For example, my mother thought that I was kicking her out of her house. We addressed her concerns through clearly labeling boxes as belonging to her, a strategy that worked for us, but that may not work for other people. AlzConnected, powered by the Alzheimer's Association, is a free online support community for everyone affected by Alzheimer's or other dementia, including people with the disease; caregivers; and family members, friends, and individuals who have lost someone to Alzheimer's.[1] The AlzConnected Caregivers Forum message board includes some great response strategies for dealing with a number of topics, including paranoia. Here are some helpful tips on responding to paranoia:

- Don't be offended or take the accusations personally. Ask what is troubling the person. Be empathetic. Remember that your loved one is not trying to cause you pain. This distorted reality is caused by changes deep in the brain. Try to understand that reality. Let the person know you care. Be reassuring.
- Don't argue or use logic to convince. Accept that this is your loved one's reality. Using logic or arguing your point with an individual who cannot process the information is not helpful. Listen and allow the individual to express his or her feelings, opinions, and thoughts. Be patient, kind, and cognizant of your tone of voice.
- Simple responses are best. The individual cannot process a detailed explanation. A long explanation will overwhelm and frustrate the individual, exacerbating matters.
- Use a diversion tactic. Change the topic of conversation or ask for help with an activity. Think of a short list of diversion tactics that you can pull out in times of paranoia or frustration. For example: *Would you look at these pictures with me on my phone? Would you like an apple as a snack? Could I help you tidy up?*
- If it's nice, buy it twice! Your loved one may frequently lose particular items and then accuse you of stealing those items. It may

help to purchase duplicates of such items. Locating the "stolen" item quickly will help diffuse a heated situation.

- Educate and learn from others. If you find a helpful response strategy, share it! Brainstorm with other caregivers to learn new ideas.[2]

Accept that some stories your loved one tells you will make no sense.

Resist the urge to fill in the gaps of a story told by your loved one with your own logic and imagination; doing so will only make you crazy. You may never know the full story of an event your loved one tells you about—even if you ask a million questions. Persons living with Alzheimer's exist in an alternate reality. While your loved one may not recall all of what just happened or a conversation that recently took place, he or she may clearly recall an obscure memory from youth. Your loved one might fill in the blanks of what they do not understand and create an entirely new story, an alternate reality. Consequently, the story you are being told may be a mix of new and old events decades apart. Resist the urge to complete the paragraph into a logical and cohesive story. What you hear may be a mix of historical and present-day occurrences.

Don't treat your loved one like a child.

Although they are not children, many of the behaviors associated with Alzheimer's are similar to behaviors of young children, such as forgetfulness, mood swings, tantrums, and problems with vocabulary. For this reason, it can be tempting to treat them like children, but they are adults. Unlike children, who learn as they grow and build upon those learnings, persons living with Alzheimer's constantly lose their knowledge. Depending upon the stage of the disease and the events, their minds may not fully comprehend what is occurring around them and how to react. They are living in an alternate reality, a parallel universe. Repeating the same thing five times is not effective when the recipient cannot remember what you said the first four times. Trying to reason with an individual is not effective when the individual is incapable of comprehending your reasoning or the overall situation around them. Being condescending or treating someone living with Alzheimer's as if he or she is a child causes frustration. Tone, body language, and word choice are important in communication. While your loved one may not remember what you said, they might remember the feelings they had when you were saying it.

Pay attention to nonverbal communication.

Sometimes your loved one may not be retelling an event, but rather trying to express a need or feeling. You cannot rely solely on verbal language. Look at your loved one's body language. Are they in physical discomfort? Can you ask a few questions about the story to see if they really need something? Pay attention to the nonverbal cues the person you are caring for is giving you. Understanding his or her feelings may be more important than the content of the conversation. Acknowledge feelings whenever possible.[3]

Communication strategies:

As Alzheimer's disease progresses, a person's ability to communicate changes.[4] Here are some strategies to assist with communication:

Changes in Communication

The following list describes communication challenges and tactics you will likely see as the disease progresses:

- Trouble identifying the correct word to use during a conversation
- Repeatedly using well-known or familiar words
- Describing an object rather than stating the name of the object
- Stopping mid-sentence or losing a train of thought
- Difficulty organizing words into a sentence
- Becoming quiet, and speaking less frequently
- Pointing to get your attention, rather than speaking[5]

Communication in the Early Stage

Although a person in the early stage of Alzheimer's disease can engage in social activities and actively participate in conversations, the individual may have difficulty finding the correct word or may repeat a question or a story. Too much stimulation may overwhelm the individual. For example, a person with Alzheimer's may have difficulty carrying on a conversation when there is a lot of background chatter or music. Here are some suggestions for successful communication in the early stage:

- Alzheimer's affects each person differently. Therefore, it is important to avoid any assumptions that the individual is not capable of communicating in a meaningful way simply because of an Alzheimer's diagnosis.
- Include people living with Alzheimer's in your conversations. Do not exclude them.
- Do not speak to a person's caregiver or companion rather than speaking directly to the individual.
- Be an active listener. Focus on the individual and listen to his or her thoughts, feelings, and needs.
- An individual living with Alzheimer's will need more time to put his or her thoughts together. Therefore, be patient. Do not interrupt or finish the individual's sentences unless the individual requests help. Give the individual enough time to respond.
- Ask for input on how your loved one would like to communicate. *Would you like some help? Are you comfortable having the TV on in the background, or would you prefer I turn it off? How would you like to communicate? Would you prefer that we talk face to face or on the phone? Would you like for me to text you?*
- Laughter is a wonderful stress reliever and lifts spirits. Although you are sad about the Alzheimer's diagnosis, it's okay to laugh. Sometimes things are just funny, such as my gracious mother greeting our family friend with "oink, oink" rather than "hello."
- Although your loved one is fading away, don't pull away yourself. You can still have meaningful conversations and experiences

during the early stage. Your support and friendship are important to your loved one. Don't turn around during the middle
and late stages and wish you had enjoyed your loved one more
during the early stage. This, quite frankly, is one of my largest
regrets.[6]

Communication in the Middle Stage

The longest stage of Alzheimer's disease, the middle stage, can last for
many years. During this stage, the individual experiences greater difficulty communicating. The individual will also require more direct care.
Suggestions for successful communication in the middle stage are listed
here:

- Be mindful of your surroundings. Limit distractions, such as
  background noises. Look for a quiet place where you can have a
  one-on-one conversation.
- Be mindful of nonverbal cues, such as body language.
- Simplify. Use short sentences. Ask questions with "yes" or "no"
  answers, or provide your loved one with a choice of two options.
  For example: *Would you like an apple or a pear? Would you prefer
  bathing before breakfast or after breakfast?* If you are explaining
  steps in a task, such as brushing one's teeth, use short, choppy
  sentences to provide step-by-step instructions. Otherwise, the
  task (and the explanation) may seem overwhelming.
- Ask one question at a time.
- Enunciate your words and speak slowly. Speak clearly. Speak in
  a calm voice.
- Establish a connection. Look the individual in the eye.
  Maintaining eye contact shows that you are interested in what
  the person is saying. Hold hands. Use the person's name during
  the conversation.
- Be patient. Your loved one will need to think about what to say,
  and it will take time to find the right words. Allow the individual
  plenty of time to respond.

- Offer encouragement. By offering reassurance, you may encourage the individual to explain his or her thoughts.

- Don't criticize or correct. Try to interpret what is being said, thinking about the context of the conversation. If the person is becoming frustrated trying to express an idea, offer a guess. Clarify what you have heard by repeating it.

- Don't treat your loved one like a child. For example, don't use baby talk. Show respect.

- Don't argue. Arguing will accomplish nothing. If you disagree with something the person said, resist the urge to argue or correct. Just let it go.

- Consider other forms of communication. Use gestures and visual cues. Try written notes. Show the person how to do something, in addition to providing verbal instruction.

- Finally, singing can be a wonderful form of verbal communication. My mother and I frequently sang together when I could not think of another activity.[7]

Communication in the Late Stage

Twenty-four-hour care is typically required during the late stage of Alzheimer's disease, which may last from several weeks to several years. To communicate, the individual may rely upon vocal sounds, facial expressions, or other forms of nonverbal communication. Here are some suggestions for successful communication in the late stage:

- Identify yourself when speaking to the person. For example, "Hi, Mom. I am your daughter, Mary, and I am here to see you."

- Communicate with the individual on the same level. If your loved one is confined to a bed, sit in a chair next to the bed so you are at eye level. This will avoid your looking down upon the person, which might feel uncomfortable for your loved one.

- Do not approach the person from behind; rather, approach the person from the front and make eye contact.

- Your loved one will have difficulty communicating with you verbally. Therefore, incorporate nonverbal communication, such as pointing or gesturing.
- Create a soothing environment. Hold hands. Make eye contact. Avoid harsh lighting. Play soothing music. Bring a nice smelling air freshener or a favorite food. These are all forms of nonverbal communication.
- Be a detective. The words being uttered by the individual may not make sense, but there is an intention or feeling behind them. *What emotion is the person trying to convey? Is the individual conveying a message through a facial expression or body language?*
- Have respect. Do not be condescending or speak as if the person is not there.
- Accept that you may not know what to say or do. Don't forget that the sounds of your voice, presence, and friendship are meaningful.[8]

Allow yourself to feel grief.

Don't make up rules for yourself about how you should or should not handle your grief. Just let the grief flow over you like a wave. Watching someone you love deteriorate is excruciatingly painful. Don't try to fight grief; just let it happen.

THINNING ZINNIAS

By Jane P. Moreland

Today I separate clumps
of seed leaves on string stems
that bend and coil for light.

I began one cold day
with an index finger punching moist earth,
the resolve of one seed to one hole.
But seeds stuck more and more to fingers,
and the pack was half full at row's end.

You see it often:
plants malformed from wrong planting,
loquats near a wall with flat backs,
frost-pruned, north yard lemons,
oaks too close leaning apart
with shorter limbs on the touching sides.

My son comes out to help,
not the big boy, not the baby,
but the one in the middle who yearns to be both,
more drawn to gardener than garden.
He uses his thumb for new holes. I hold
pale sprouts upright as he tamps in soil,
and we allow each its light and space.

Chapter 4

Supporting Children through the Alzheimer's Journey

Our family ambulance, a maroon Honda Odyssey, frequently transported dying houseplants to Dr. Grandma Jane, who tirelessly nursed our patients back to health on her colorful ceramic tiled hospital table on the back porch. My boys and I would imitate ambulance sirens during our brief transport, show the doctor each patient and wait anxiously for her expert medical diagnosis.

Dr. Grandma Jane was always very serious. Too much water. Needs more soil. Not enough sun. Too much sun. I think I can save this one. I am not sure about the other . . . It may be too late. I am sorry for your loss. Occasionally, the doctor would shoot me a disappointed glance, like I imagined a pediatrician might look at the parent of a neglected child.

We visited our patients and Dr. Grandma Jane often. However, on this day, not only did Dr. Grandma Jane seem completely oblivious about her most critical medical role, but she also had no idea as to the whereabouts of the patients!

My son was confused. He wanted answers. I was unprepared. I explained that Grandma Jane was ill. She would forget things. In my naïveté, I said that she didn't forget the important things—like who we were or where she lived. *How could she forget those things?* Just some other things that really in the scheme of life weren't all that important—like her role as Dr. Grandma Jane, Plant Doctor. Or, if the fern or sunflower were ill. *I mean, honestly, who really cares?*

In retrospect, not my best Mother Moment.

"Mare, when will your father be home? Why isn't he here? Where did he go?" she asked a few minutes later. Shaking and confused, my lovely son stated quite clearly and deliberately: "I think the fact that your husband is dead is probably pretty important, don't you?! Maybe important, like where you live is important! You said she didn't forget anything important," he said as he turned to me. He was always very smart. I apologized. He was correct.

Being in the sandwich generation means that you support those who need you both young and old. My son needed a rational explanation. He also needed to understand why his mother had provided him with false information. What would happen next and how to handle it. What to expect. My mother needed understanding, patience, and empathy. She was confused and hurt. She also needed the truth, or some version of the truth, even if she did not understand it, and it was painful for me to deliver.

Honestly, this is the first time I have considered what I may have needed at that moment. At that moment, it did not matter. What mattered was the bread, and I was the meat.

Being in the sandwich generation means that you put your needs, thoughts, and feelings on hold. A hug, a warm word, someone to ask how you are doing. It's not that you forget these needs. As humans, we need these things. People in the sandwich generation, at least people like myself, learn how to hit pause. Pause because others more vulnerable than you, and those you love, require instant attention.

Hitting pause implies that you will eventually hit play. But life has a way of not allowing you to watch the end of the show, and inevitably, you move on to the next episode interested to see what will transpire, thinking you will eventually go back, but you don't.

In retrospect, I have learned that never hitting play and never dealing with those feelings does not make them go away. Quite the opposite occurs, and they resurface with a vengeance, hijacking your brain and leading to much worse situations. They come out sideways in poor decisions about your personal life, overuse of alcohol, or depression, threatening your happiness and overall mental health. Watch the entire show. Seek out someone to talk to or journal. Deal with the feelings, even though it's really the last thing you think you have time for.

My children appreciate my relationship with my mother, but they do not understand it. When she was lucid and herself, they were too young to remember it. As her disease progressed and her mind deteriorated, she did not remember them. My children also do not remember most interactions with their grandfather. I was fortunate to have enjoyed my grandparents until I was in my mid-twenties.

When we look at old home movies, my sons see characters in the movies to whom they relate. Everything seems familiar, but they are not there. They do not know the people in the home movies, but their jokes are funny. There is a sense of familiarity. They have seen home movies of my mother and are shocked by how in charge and confident she seems. She is not the woman with the miscolored hair and chipped red nails who can't remember she wants to order shrimp for lunch. She is the woman creating the menu and telling everyone where to sit!

I want them to understand how talented, funny, and bright their grandmother was, but they never will. To them, I think she may always be the person who lived on the dreaded memory care floor. They may vaguely recall taking our plants to Dr. Grandma Jane, but the memory is hazy.

I know they will remember seeing how much I loved their grand-mother, but I do not think they will ever really appreciate the beauty and talent of my mother. They may read her poetry later in life and appreciate it, but they will not know the warmth of her hug, the beauty of her smile, her kind words, or her excellent sense of humor. She will never beat them at Scrabble. When she passed, I think my children felt guilty that they didn't feel more, but *how could they feel more?* This was no fault of theirs, and hopefully they understood. *How can you mourn someone you never really knew?* Alzheimer's is a thief.

I want them to remember things that I do about loved ones who have passed—Mom feeding them on their highchair at her house. Her extra handful of snacks. Their grandmother on their dad's side introducing me to bananas in baby cereal. The song she used to sing before they ate ("mmm, mmm, good, mmm, mmm, good"). The first moment of ice cream, which my father encouraged me to order even though I insisted my son was not quite ready for ice cream. The way my mom held them. How she played with them and read them books. How she sometimes just stared at them in amazement and awe—whether they were in my arms or hers.

My children are almost grown men. *How do I instill in them the love she felt? How do I make them know that they are loved by multiple generations, when these generations have passed?* They are part of something bigger. They only know their mother, father, one grandfather, and a small number of aunts and uncles and cousins. How do I make sure they know that many, many people love them—that they are supported by many generations. That many people want them to succeed, be happy, love, live—whether these people are here with us or have passed on to something else. *How do I show them that in some ways all those prior generations are still here?* Because they are! I know they are! Just because your people move on doesn't mean they stop loving you. They always love you—even when they are gone. You are always part of the broader family. Their love remains, and we continue as part of them. *How do we draw on that strength when we are here alive on earth? How can I show this love and support to my kids?*

Talking to Children About Alzheimer's

Be open with your children about Alzheimer's.
Talk to children about Alzheimer's; it is important for children to know that the behaviors of loved ones with Alzheimer's are not because of them, but rather because of changes taking place deep within their brains. Alzheimer's affects everyone differently, and it affects the entire family, including children. The age, stage of development, and personality of a child will affect how each child reacts to learning that a loved one is living

44

with Alzheimer's. Just like adults, it may take children time to adjust to the news. They may also not fully appreciate what Alzheimer's is or its effects. Children are intuitive and will likely realize something is wrong before being told. Children will notice the stress and sadness in other family members and wonder if they have done something to cause it. Understanding that unusual behavior is due to a disease and not something they caused may come as a relief. Therefore, it is important to have an open and honest conversation about the Alzheimer's diagnosis, rather than trying to spare children of the emotional turmoil of Alzheimer's. Allow children to express their feelings, listen carefully, and make sure they know you will not judge them for what they say.

Remind children that they are not the cause of forgetfulness, anger, or frustration.

Explain that a loved one's forgetfulness or repetition of the same question is the disease, not due to something the child did or did not do. For example, Grandma Jane is not repeating the same question every five minutes because she did not like your answer. She literally cannot remember that she already asked you the question! If Grandma Jane is angry or upset, it is likely because she is frustrated, not due to something that you did or said. Acknowledge that some events, things their loved one says, and things they do may seem odd, even funny.

Encourage children to notice and celebrate the things the person with dementia can still do.

For example, a game of Monopoly may no longer be realistic, but listening to music, singing a song together, a very simple puzzle, a brief walk, looking through photo albums, or coloring a picture together might be enjoyable. Games like Connect Four, UNO, or Spot It! can be fun. The Alzheimer's Association has a helpful site for kids and teens that includes explanations, videos, and a list of fifty activities to do when spending time with a family member or friend in the middle or late stages of Alzheimer's, as well as numerous educational materials for kids and teens.[1] Keep in mind that outings and activities need not be complicated. Don't put pressure on yourself to have an "outing" like to a museum or a movie, which might be overstimulating. Simple works.

Remind children that their loved one still deserves respect.

The Alzheimer's Society UK has a website with helpful suggestions for how to talk about dementia with children and young people, as well as short videos that you can watch together.[2] Remind yourself that you are a role model for your children and that they will look to you for cues on how to treat a loved one with an illness.

Use storytelling as a communication tool.

If you feel uncomfortable about talking to a child or don't quite know what to say, books and videos are an excellent bridge for doing so.

There are several children's books that you can read together about Alzheimer's or dementia, as few of which are listed below.

- *What's Happening to Grandpa?* Maria Shriver, Little, Brown & Co., 2004.
- *Still My Grandma,* Veronique Van Den Abeele and Claude K. Dubois (illustrator), Eerdman's Books for Young Readers, 2007.
- *Grandma and Me: A Kid's Guide for Alzheimer's and Dementia,* Beatrice Tauber PsyD, Morgan James Kids, 2017.
- *The Remember Balloons,* Jessie Oliveros, Simon & Schuster Books for Young Readers, 2018.
- *Remember, Grandma?* Laura Langston, Viking Juvenile, 2004.
- *Why Did Grandma Put Her Underwear in the Refrigerator?* Max Wallack, Carolyn Given, CreateSpace, 2013.

The Alzheimer's Society UK YouTube Channel is an excellent resource for videos.[3] The Alzheimer's Association website includes a number of videos specifically for teens.[4]

Wearing His Feet

By Jane P. Moreland

Even now, fragments of my grandfather appear
in sock drawers and in the toes of Christmas stockings:
silver belt buckle, copper ashtray, ceramic tree stump
for wooden matches. It's my mother's mission:
    Don't let any of us forget him.

His bequests are sufficient: stubborn streak
that pushed him on, mean streak when pushed to limits,
imperious second toes on pale, blue-veined feet.
    Looking down, I see thin skin stretched
over knobby joints, his tarsals, metatarsals, phalanges.

One treasure he told me, how on a starry night in 1910,
    from flat on field stubble, he saw the blaze
    of Halley's Comet. The next night, from a dormer,
he saw it again at a juncture of eaves through limbs
of sparse magnolia, still coming straight for him.

When the comet returned years after he was gone,
    I had to see it. City lights were too bright,
so I set out on back roads. I found it over the Gulf,
    silver torch hurtling velvet sky. I wondered
    if it would snuff into the sea. That night,
    I knew his feet were mine for a reason:
I should step where he stepped. It's how I'll find him.
    At the ladders to heaven, some angel will say,
anyone who saw Halley's Comet, come this way.

Chapter 5

Maximizing the Ability to Support Your Loved One: The Gift of Documentation

I believe the best gift my parents gave me was the gift of documentation. I remember it well: the year was 2009, two years before Mom's diagnosis. My father called me downstairs to discuss a matter with him and my mother. I sat on the bench in front of the fireplace next to his chair wondering why I was in trouble. Calling me downstairs to have a serious conversation with them was extremely unusual. He handed me a yellow envelope of documents. I opened the envelope. It was full of legal documents. My father carefully explained each one, while my mother occasionally interjected her opinion.

A medical power of attorney. A directive to physicians relating to end-of-life care. A financial power of attorney. Wills for each parent. Other documents. All the documents one would need in Texas to care for another person. They both asked me if I would be their executors and attorney in fact, in the event one passed before the other. They carefully explained why they had selected me as first in line to oversee each of them. After all, I was the lawyer in the family. I also lived within biking distance, less than a mile away. Of course, I agreed.

Although I did not fully appreciate the significance of the documentation at the time, in retrospect, for me this was a gift. I never had to undergo the stress and expense of a proceeding to be appointed as the guardian for my mother. I was able to take care of her as I thought necessary considering her wishes. I was able to seamlessly gain access to her financial accounts and speak with her medical doctors. The documentation allowed me to refill her prescriptions, manage her money, pay her bills, file her tax returns, hire caregivers, sell her house, sign a lease at the assisted care facility, hire hospice, and do so many other countless things. Despite your loved one's mental incapacity and your familial relationship, no one will talk to you unless you are legally authorized by your loved one or a court to do so. Not even the cable TV provider.

One thing that surprised me was the way different care facilities and medical professionals interpreted the medical documentation. Additionally, although I thought I had all documentation, sometimes I was required to sign additional "do not resuscitate" documents. The hospital might have a form to execute. The nursing home had a Texas state out-of-hospital form. Some forms required two witnesses. Some a notary. Some a simple signature. At least this is what I experienced. A new conversation occurred each time Mom was admitted to the hospital, which is not how you want to spend your time when your loved one is ill! Although I understand healthcare personnel were following required procedures, it just added to the stress. Informing nurses and administrator of the "do not resuscitate" made me feel like a mommy hater, yet I merely was ensuring my mother's wishes were respected. There is no reason to feel bad about that. In fact, it was good that healthcare personnel asked so many questions, because it demonstrated that they wanted to have clarity in the event of an emergency. Once I accepted that this is simply part of the process of admitting a person to a hospital or a nursing home, my stress subsided.

Mom never wanted to be on permanent life-sustaining support. To me, this seemed quite black and white, but as it turns out, there are many shades of gray. I first encountered this when Mom had a urinary tract infection and was admitted into the hospital. The nurse asked me if Mom had a directive to physicians. I provided her a copy. Of course, I had to also sign a hospital form. It is one thing for my mother to sign a form stating she does not want life support. It is another thing for me to sign a document stating I do not want efforts taken to save my mother's life. Frankly, it made me feel like a crappy kid.

Then, the questions began from the nurse who explained to me she just wanted to have a clear understanding. *If she were not breathing and needed to be on a ventilator, would that be okay? Well, do you think she would eventually come off the ventilator?* "Permanently being on a ventilator" to a layperson seems straightforward, but in the days of COVID, it is not. *If she cannot eat for herself, do you agree to a stomach plug? Well, without it, she would starve to death, wouldn't she?* I don't want my mom to starve to death. However, when a body shuts down before death, the person no longer eats. *Is that starving to death?* As a layperson, I don't know.

I now occasionally invite friends or acquaintances with loved ones living with Alzheimer's or other forms of dementia to visit with me on my back porch and talk about their experiences. After listening to their story, I always ask if their loved ones have provided anyone with the gift of documentation. This is a key question to ask early in the disease because only individuals with mental and legal capacity can enter legally binding documents. When a loved one falls ill, medical personnel are typically the first ones called, and understandably so. However, to give the gift of documentation, one must also seek legal advice.

From speaking with friends and acquaintances, I have learned that many parents resist signing these types of documents for a variety of reasons. For example, they may believe the person requesting the documentation has ulterior motives. For some people a direct conversation with a trusted neutral party, such as a doctor or lawyer, about the necessity and purpose of such documentation has been helpful.

Assuming you are fortunate enough to have the gift of documentation, you will need to understand the documentation. There are several strategies for doing so. You could discuss with the attorney who drafted the documentation and your loved one's primary care doctor in detail to clearly understand the documentation earlier than you perhaps need to so that you aren't caught off guard when these questions arise. Some law schools and State Bar associations sponsor elder care clinics. The Association of American Retired Persons, AARP, is another resource.

Local senior centers, hospitals, and physicians may also be able to assist. Ask the expert to walk you through the medical power of attorney and directive to physician's documents and explain what it all means. Talk to your doctor about medical risks and what could happen next. Be specific. Ideally, however painful, you could discuss these matters with your loved one at the early stages of Alzheimer's. If your loved one is no longer capable of making these types of decisions, then talk to family. *What would your loved one want? Is everyone on the same page?* There is nothing worse than making a tough decision with pure intentions and then being criticized for it.

Preparing for the Legal Issues that May Arise

Put legal documentation in place.

To the extent you are able, make sure the required legal documentation is in place to allow you to care for your loved one and ensure that his or her wishes are respected. The law is very strict about who can receive medical information and make medical decisions. Healthcare providers will not talk to you about your loved one's care unless you are legally authorized. Banks will not provide you with access to your loved one's accounts unless you are legally authorized, even if the purpose is to pay your loved one's bills. Having the documentation in place makes caring for your loved one easier and less expensive and is necessary before the need arises, which means you must plan ahead. For these documents to be legally binding, your loved one must have "legal capacity." In simple terms, this means that your loved one must have the ability to understand and appreciate the documentation and its consequences. At a certain point in the disease your loved one will lack legal capacity. If the documentation is not in place or your loved one is no longer legally capable, you may need to petition a court to become the legal guardian of your loved one.

List of important documents:

The purpose of legal documentation, such as wills, advance directives, and powers of attorney, is to document how your affairs will be handled in the future and who will be legally authorized to make decisions on your behalf when you are unable to do so. The specific requirements for these documents will vary by state law. The National Institute on Aging and Alzheimer's Association have resource pages concerning medical and financial documentation. The list below—"Important Legal Documents You May Need as You Age"—is provided by the National Institute on Aging and provides a general overview of what is required; however, keep in mind that what is necessary will vary by state:

- A last will and testament is a legal document that sets forth who will receive your property (such as your house, your assets, your car, etc.) after your death. A will can also describe your wishes regarding the care of your minor children after you die.
- An advance directive is a legal document that explains how you would like medical decisions to be made if you are unable to make these decisions yourself because you are too sick. Common types of advance directives are (1) a living will and (2) a durable power of attorney for health care.
  - Although the names are similar, a living will is different than a last will and testament. Through a living will, you maintain a say in your health care even if you are too ill to make your wishes known. In a living will, you state the types of medical care you do or do not want. For example, if you do not want life-prolonging procedures administered or continued if there is not probability of your survival, you can state this in the living will. Having a living will can make it easier for family members to make tough healthcare decisions for you, because your family will carry out decisions that you have already made. A living will also preserves your voice in your own end-of-life care.

- A durable power of attorney for health care is a legal document in which you name the person you would like to make medical decisions for you if you are unable to make them yourself. Before signing the document, you should confirm that the person named to make medical decisions on your behalf is willing to make those decisions for you.

- In addition to legal documentation relating to your medical care, you may also want to put in place legal documentation governing your financial or other matters.
  - A general power of attorney is a legal document in which you give someone else the authority to make plans and decisions for you; however, this power ceases if you are incapable of making decisions by yourself.
  - A durable power of attorney is a legal document in which you give someone else the authority to act on your behalf for any legal task. Unlike a general power of attorney, this document remains in effect if you become incapable of making your own decisions.[1]

The National Hospice and Palliative Care Organization provides free advance directives and instructions for each state that are downloadable from the organization's website.[2]

Provide copies to key people and make sure documents are easily accessible.

Apart from having the requisite documentation, it is also important that key people, such as doctors, are provided with a copy of the relevant documentation. Provide a copy to family members, or at least make sure they know how to locate the documentation. Keep your loved one's critical documents (insurance card, medical power of attorney, etc.) together in a secure location that will be easy to find if you need to produce the documents in a hurry.

Create a summary of important information.

Create a summary with names and contact details of doctors, pharmacies, and other important contacts and essential information for family members in case the primary caregiver is not available. Keep family members in the loop about your vacation or work travel. Here is a starting list of items to include in your summary:

- Personal information
  - Full legal name
  - Address
  - Social Security number
  - Date of birth
  - Place of birth
  - Names and contact details of spouse and children
  - Employer details
  - Military and education details
  - Memberships in groups, such as AARP
- Medical information
  - Medical providers (primary, dentist, other)
  - Preferred pharmacy
  - Current medication list
  - Insurance information
- Legal information
  - Contact details for legal or other providers
  - List of critical documentation (living will, powers of attorney, will, etc.)
  - Location of critical documentation
- Financial information
  - List of bank and savings accounts, including names of people on the accounts
  - List of assets
  - Sources of income, including any IRAs, pension plans, interest revenue, 401(k)s, etc.
  - List of any loans or debts

- ✦ Medicare/Medicaid/Social Security information
- ✦ Insurance information (medical, vision, dental, Medicare supplemental insurance, long-term care, home, auto, umbrella, etc.)
- ✦ Car title and registration
- ✦ Copy of most recent tax return
- ✦ Credit and debit card details
- ✦ Names of providers, such as cell phone, electricity, natural gas, water, etc.
- ✦ Real estate documentation (lease agreement, deed to home, mortgage details)
- ✦ Location of safe deposit box and key, if any
- Pet information
  - ✦ Names, types, and ages of pets
  - ✦ Veterinarian details
  - ✦ Pet insurance, if any[3]

Plan for the future.

Ideally, your loved one would have discussed end-of-life care with his or her medical doctor or directly informed you of his or her end-of-life wishes.[4] However, this is not always realistic. Discuss your loved one's wishes about end-of-life care with his or her doctor. Ask questions. Be specific. When caring for someone with Alzheimer's, it is tempting to live only in the present moment. If you train your mind to look at the horizon, not your feet walking the ground, you can avoid much stress. Plan one step ahead. Ask your doctor—*What's next? What do we need to be thinking about as a family in terms of the next stage of the illness? What are some things you have seen families struggle with in terms of medical care?* Communicate. Discuss these matters with relevant family members or friends who have a say in your loved one's care. Planning one step ahead can be the secret to sanity with Alzheimer's. Knowing the answers before they are asked is much better than finding out the answers urgently in response to an emergency, particularly with such weighty and critical issues. Having a longer-term plan can provide you with a sense of control over the future, which might lower your stress level.

Have strategies if your loved one resists putting documentation in place.

For a variety of reasons, your loved one may resist putting documentation in place that allows you to act on his or her behalf. He or she may see this act as you "taking control" over their lives or an attempt to steal from them or harm them in some way. Your loved one may not wish to share intimate details, such as a medication list, list of assets or bank account details. The following suggestions may be helpful:

- Explain to your loved one why you are concerned and why the documentation is necessary. Your intent is not to take over their life, but rather to be prepared for when they need your assistance. If legal formalities have not been taken, you will not be able to care for him or her when they need you, and you want to make sure his or her wishes are respected.

- It is not realistic to wait until the documentation is needed. By that time, your loved one may not have the required legal capacity.

- Not putting documentation in place will inevitably be more expensive and require a more complicated legal process, such as the appointment of a guardian. Additionally, if a guardianship is the only option, there is no guarantee as to who would be selected as the guardian. The guardian could even be a stranger unknown to your loved one. There may also be fees associated with the guardianship, diminishing the funds available for your loved one's long-term care.

- Offer to make an appointment with a neutral third party, such as a medical doctor or an elder care lawyer, who can clearly explain the purpose of an advance directive, power of attorney, and other relevant documentation. Perhaps you have a family friend who has put such documentation in place. Hearing an explanation from an expert or a friend rather than one's own child can be helpful.

- Remind your loved one that he or she can place restrictions in the documentation on your abilities. For example, the power of attorney provided by my parents restricted me from making certain types of gifts. It was not a "blank check."

If your loved one is not receptive, you could take a phased approach. For example, your loved one could provide permission to Medicare or his or her doctor or lawyer for them to talk to the caregiver directly, as needed, because there may be questions about insurance coverage or a bill. You could assist your loved one in paying bills every month and ask for consent in advance for you to talk to the bank or credit card company. Once your parent or other loved one sees that you are genuinely trying to assist, he or she might be more receptive to something more comprehensive and formal.

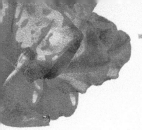

STEPPING DOWN THE LIGHT

By Jane P. Moreland

The driveway swept, my father's standing
in a grass sea, well off the shore of concrete.
He leans on his broom and watches
the red blaze of sun through the pine horizon
along the back fence, fiery end of a day.

The broom is new to replace the one
worn with what he does every evening,
that sweeping of leaves, twigs, bugs
from the driveway, and long after that,
imaginary dust, things he sees that we don't.

I call his name, and he looks around, stranded,
like days we'd be fishing in the Gulf,
watching waves for what swam with the porpoises.
We'd forget the tide until it was almost too late
to come in on tiptoes, tackle held high.

He can't decide which way to move,
and just now, he can't call my name.
These days, he knows me in flashes,
unexpected drops of moonlight spilled down
a dark leaf, sudden shot stars
in velvet sky, like out of the vast blue
he might remember to tell me
about the tiny silver key in his desk
or to return a book I borrowed years ago.

I'm at the edge of the driveway,
where the sun has made a puzzle
of bright stairs fit to shadows
at the corrugated edge of the carport roof.
I hold out my hand, become the rope he threw
when the tide came in as we waded
on different sand bars. He takes my arm,
and together we walk, skirting shadow,
down deep light steps toward home.

Chapter 6

Choosing the Best Types of Care

It was clear my mother needed additional help. She also needed companionship. Therefore, I took my mother to a dementia day care for a tour. I had met with the staff before we arrived and provided a bit of background. Many people living with dementia had "jobs" at the center. The center had agreed that Mom could teach a writing class. She could read her poetry and talk about writing. I was very excited and thought she would like the idea. I thought she might enjoy the activities and make some new friends.

During our meeting she politely told the representative that writing for her was a solitary task. In the parking lot she curtly informed me that she did not belong at That Place. "I will not be returning." "This place is not for me, Mare." "I don't belong here."

Alzheimer's is just so confusing. How is this place not for you?! You think your dead (and retired) husband of fifty years ran off with someone he met on a business trip in New York City, a place neither of you have been in decades. You think you met Dad at your sorority house in college while you were manning the phones!

But she said it was not, so of course, we never returned.

The same things happened at an Alzheimer's event at the church. This time there were ugly hats for everyone to wear as a fun diversion. I cannot erase from my memory the picture of my mother with a scowl on her face like a petulant kid wearing a truly hideous hat. Not returning.

These outings were my attempts at providing my mother with a social life. However, I think she was happy and comfortable just continuing her regular routine at home. Several years later I would see her at the nursing home laughing with her group of friends, and I wondered if I should have pushed her more to be more social earlier. *Would pushing her out of her comfort zone have provided her with a better quality of life?* Second-guessing and revisiting decisions already made are not helpful. As I tell my kids, all you can do is try your best, and if you have genuinely done your best, you can feel proud.

My attempts at incorporating adult day care or church outings were unsuccessful. If she left the house, Mom would need someone to drive her to those places, and I would be at work. I briefly considered quitting my job and dedicating my time to my mother and my children, but this was not a realistic idea. I was the primary breadwinner. I also had worked hard in law school and as a lawyer, and there were goals I wanted to accomplish for myself. I considered moving my mother into my house. However, my house was not large enough for an additional person, and Mom would still need assistance and companionship. I considered moving my family into Mom's house. Mom loved her home and had lived there for almost forty years. However, my children and I loved our home. Wherever Mom lived, I worried about exposing my children to twenty-four hours a day of Alzheimer's. After discussing the matter with family, we decided to hire a companion to visit Mom's house for a few hours several times per week. In our view, the best care for our mother would be in her familiar environment.

How do you find such a person? How do you trust someone to look after your mother? Unlike a small child, she was an adult. *Would she accept having a new friend she did not select?* We contacted acquaintances we knew had loved ones living with Alzheimer's and other forms of dementia. Friends posted notes on church bulletin boards. Being a lawyer who traveled quite frequently for work and a single parent, I was intimately familiar with the childcare scene. I called out to acquaintances and childcare agencies to see if anyone could recommend someone for my mother. However, with very rare exceptions (and mostly due to a need for an income) people who looked after babies and young children did not want to look after Jane. In retrospect, I see that contacting my childcare resources was a terrible idea. People living with Alzheimer's are not children. They benefit from care from people who understand the disease and know how to effectively communicate with them as adults. We gathered all the names we could find and scheduled a marathon day of interviews.

How upsetting. The woman who taught me my colors, my numbers. Who potty-trained me and watched me sit on the sidelines during every middle school athletic event, but never mentioned my lack of athletic ability, needed a glorified babysitter. "You are the best athlete in the family!" She was always honest. Sadly, the bench-warming daughter was the best athlete of the Moreland children.

The person who taught me to "pay myself first" and automatically move a portion of my salary each month to savings. "You will be surprised how much it will grow, and you will be used to living on less." A decorated poet. A fiction contest judge. A master of Scrabble. *How can I be interviewing "friends" for the Master of Scrabble?* But there I was, sitting at my dining room table, talking about who would be the best companion for Mom. Paying someone to spend time with my beloved mother.

We located two people: Liz and Kathy. Liz and Kathy had worked together in the past, but now were caring for different people. Liz would come to the house for a few hours on certain days and Kathy on other days. We clicked. They were empathetic and loving. They understood Alzheimer's. They wanted to partner with us in the care for our mother. To them, it was not just a job, but a meaningful relationship that would be formed. They knew she would die. They cared and understood preserving dignity. Trust would be built. They were interested in who Mom was as a person and wanted to get to know her, not just babysit her. They appreciated that Mom was someone who had a disease and understood that she deserved respect. They understood that despite Alzheimer's, there were still laughs to be had and experiences to enjoy. They understood that Mom was a unique person, not a walking death sentence.

My mother had purchased a long-term care policy in middle age for which she paid an impressively reasonable premium. She purchased every possible rider: the policy paid a certain amount per day for care even if you used less. Once you entered a facility, there was no premium. The coverage did not stop after a defined number of years; rather, it continued to pay throughout her life. My mother lived with Alzheimer's for over a decade. As the person who managed her finances, I estimate that, by the date of her death, the long-term care insurance company had paid upwards of $1 million for her care. I am thankful for her foresight and for the policy every day. It allowed us to focus on Mom's care, rather than the cost of Mom's care.

The 2020 Genworth Cost of Care Summary provides a high-level overview of the 2020 national median rates for various types of care settings. There are three types of care settings described in the survey: in-home, community, and facility. Within the in-home sector, there are two predominate health services: homemaker and home health aide. Communities include services such as adult day care. Facilities give the most options but can be the most expensive. These options include assisted living facilities and nursing home care. All these care settings provide different services. These services are detailed below.

Homemaker services are services rendered in the home that offer help for household tasks that are harder for your loved one to handle alone. It is a "hands-off" care approach. Tasks that homemaker services usually handle are cooking, cleaning, and running errands. The average annual median cost of homemaker services is $53,768.

Home health aide services are more "hands-on" care rendered in the home. This is a more expensive type of care than homemaker services, but does not include medical care. The average annual median cost detailed in Genworth's summary for a non-Medicare certified licensed agency is $54,912.

Community facilities, such as adult day care, come in various models. They offer supervision, socialization, and structured activities in a community-based, protective setting. Some—but not all—programs include more personal care items, such as food, transportation, and medical management. The average annual median cost of adult day care is $19,240.

Facilities provide the most options for your loved one. The different options—assisted living facilities and a semi-private or private room at a nursing home—address different needs. Nursing homes often have more supervision and care than assisted living facilities. Residents have personalized, twenty-four-hour nursing care and supervision, room, and board, as well as staff to help with medication, therapies, and rehabilitation. According to the summary, the annual median cost for a semi-private room at a nursing home is $93,075; a private room at a nursing home has an annual median cost of $105,850. If one thinks a more intermediate level of care better suits their loved one's needs, assisted living may be a good option. It still provides personal care and health services for a lower annual median cost of $51,600.[1]

Who can afford this type of care? What do people do when they do not have a long-term care policy or other resources? There must be a better answer. As I am terrified of contracting Alzheimer's, I have since purchased my own "hybrid" long-term care policy, which can be used for either life insurance after my death or long-term care during my life. The policy was incredibly expensive and offers less coverage. The policies from my mother's era are no longer available. I think of all the wonderful people with the same disease who did not have this benefit. My hope is that my children will not be saddled by a choice between my safety and happiness and their dreams and desires. Dealing with an Alzheimer's parent is surely enough. I feel for families who are not so lucky. Yet something else to thank Mom for. She always was a planner.

According to the Alzheimer's Association 2021 Alzheimer's Disease Facts and Figures, over 11 million unpaid caregivers in the United States provided an estimated 15.3 billion hours valued at nearly $257 billion.[2] I have talked to friends and acquaintances who struggle to afford care for their loved one. Selling a home, borrowing against a life insurance policy, taking leave under the Family and Medical Leave Act (FMLA), long-term care riders to existing life insurance policies, annuities, reverse mortgages, home equity loans, and Medicaid are possible strategies mentioned during our conversations. You might want to also investigate whether your employer has any benefits that might be helpful, such as access to an adviser under an employee assistance program (EAP). Some of those in the sandwich generation are also paying for childcare and school tuition. Forget about saving for college. Many have disagreements with siblings about who should provide care, how much care, and whether that family caregiver should be paid. When siblings live in another city this becomes even more complicated, as the out-of-town sibling at least at some point in time is accused or thought of as not doing enough. Family members who are career-focused can be seen as selfish. I often remind myself how incredibly fortunate we were to have a different situation.

Apart from verifying Mom's illness through her doctor, one of the first steps of the long-term care coverage was insurance company approval of our chosen caregivers. Although they had spent years caring for people with various forms of dementia, according to the insurance company, they lacked formal training and were not qualified. I interpreted this as meaning not enough course certificates. I told them to go home and find every certificate of a course, certification (such as CPR certifications), and reference letters that they could locate. Fortunately, the Alzheimer's Association offered an online training and certification course. Surely, a certification from the Alzheimer's Association combined with their other documentation would suffice. To my delight, the caregivers were approved!

My mother was not happy about having strangers in her home. She was furious with her children for thinking she needed assistance. In some ways, she reminded me of myself as a young teenager trying to assert my power and independence. In response to her children inviting strangers to her home, she banished Liz and Kathy to an upstairs room of the house. Occasionally, she would quietly creep up the stairs to check on them and see if they were still there and what they were doing. As they were trying to establish trust, they followed her instructions. Had it not been for their intimate knowledge of the disease, being exiled and then spied upon would surely have been offensive!

When I checked in to make sure my mother had taken her medication, she would open her mouth wide and stick out her tongue like you might see in a movie scene of a patient in a mental health facility. How dare her children control her life. She was the adult. They had no right. They were mere children. She would show them by opening her mouth widely and sticking out her tongue.

During the period of banishment, Liz, Kathy, and I got to work. With a Wi-Fi hotspot, Alzheimer's Certification School began. Liz was delighted to take a class and test her knowledge. She was already taking online college level courses and confidently began her studies knowing she would be successful and hoping to learn something new.

Kathy was nervous. School was not her strength. She wanted to know if this was necessary. She wanted to help us, she liked Jane, but she didn't know if she could. A serious case of test anxiety. I assured her that all would work out well, she would pass, and at the end of the day, she would have another tool in her tool kit that would help her in the future. We would take the course again and again and again until she passed. Apart from that, what else would she do during upstairs exile? Kathy agonized at every multiple-choice response—she pressed the key and peeked with one eye, afraid of what she would see. When she got an answer right, she squealed with surprise and joy. When an answer was wrong, she barked at the computer screen and demanded to know why. Watching and listening to her taking the course was as entertaining as a movie.

In addition to ensuring our caregivers were qualified, there was an assessment of my mother. Apart from forms completed by doctors, the insurance company sent someone to the house to meet my mother in person and assess her mental ability. Fortunately, they were happy for me to also attend if I did not interfere. I explained to my mother that this was necessary for her insurance coverage. She was not happy. We eventually learned that she would do anything we said her primary doctor thought was necessary for her health. She always had cared greatly about her health and respected her doctor. So, as it turns out, her doctor wanted her to take this assessment; it was good for her health. Well, if he wanted her to speak with this person, she would begrudgingly do it.

"Okay, Jane, can you repeat the names of animals I told you a few minutes ago?" "Now I want you to count backwards by threes from one hundred." "Jane, do you dress yourself?" "Do you go to the bathroom by yourself?" The questions went on and on for what seemed like an eternity. Occasionally, my mother shot me looks with raised eyebrows of surprise. Sometimes she was offended. Slits of eyes with furrowed eyebrows shot looks of disgust and a huff my way before answering. "Yes, I most certainly do go to the bathroom by myself!"

She politely deflected questions she could not answer with charm and a smile. "I don't really think that's necessary, do you?" "Oh, Ms. Moreland, it is necessary." "Oh, surely no!" She would wave her hand, laugh, and toss her head back. "Why don't you count backward, and I will listen?" At one point, she suggested that they just break the rules. "Why not? Let's live. Let's just say we counted backward . . . and not do it!" By the end of the visit, the interviewer was blushing.

Next was the elimination period. The elimination period is a waiting period before the benefits take effect. Like a deductible, it is a period when you pay, and the insurance company does not. During the elimination period and beyond, meticulous time records must be kept. Liz and Kathy were required to sign a fraud waiver for every weekly paycheck. Front and back of canceled checks must be copied and submitted. No wire payments were allowed. It amounted to a lot of paper jams in my printer and reoccurring orders of expensive toner. Hopefully, the insurance companies have now modernized a bit.

These documentation requirements continued until my mother moved to a facility. Once in the facility, the staff handled all insurance forms for which you paid, at least in our case, a one-hundred-dollar processing fee per month on top of the price of your room and expenses. Not to sound obnoxious, but I wish I could have charged a hundred dollars a month for my invoicing services.

Assessing Your Loved One's Needs

Alzheimer's care is highly individualized.
An individual's caregiving needs change as Alzheimer's disease progresses. What works for an individual with mild cognitive impairment will not work when that person experiences middle or late-stage Alzheimer's dementia. Personalities differ. What works for one person may not work for another.[3] Our caregiver journey lasted eight and a half years. We started with in-home health aide services for a limited number of hours on certain days per week. We gradually increased this care to twenty-four hours a day, supplementing with an agency. The next step was a move to an assisted living floor at a nursing home. Our final caregiving stage was on the memory care floor of the nursing home.

Your care plan may consist of a matrix of different types of care.
There are many different types of care available, including adult day care centers, home care, and residential facilities. When looking at care options, use all your resources. Church bulletin boards, agencies, word of mouth and any other avenues you can think of. You may be able to build a care team from friends and family. There are many online tools and calendar resources that help families share tasks and get organized.[4] Your care plan may consist of a combination of families, friends, adult day care and other resources. All these resources form an overall care team for your loved one.

Share information about your loved one with care resources, and be receptive to learning new strategies.
Educate others about your loved one. Tell them about his or her life, where he or she was born, how many children he or she has. This type of information might be helpful for communication. Your care resources are your partners. All team members may not know your loved one as you do, but other members may have a lot of experience with Alzheimer's

that you do not. You can learn from each other. Adult day care centers, nursing homes, and churches often offer free seminars and host support groups. Although it is tempting to tell yourself you do not have time to attend these events, they are an excellent place to learn new strategies and commiserate with others in similar circumstances.

Reassess your care plan as the disease progresses.

Regardless of the type of care, it is important to identify the type of assistance your loved one needs and continuously reevaluate whether needs have changed. For example, take these into consideration: Does your loved one need medical care, or just companionship? Does the caregiver need to drive, help with shopping, or prepare meals? Is wandering a concern? Is your loved one either forgetting to eat or eating lunch multiple times per day? Are there safety hazards in the kitchen that need to be addressed?

Tips and suggested questions relating to long-term care policies:

- You will be assigned an insurance adjuster. Have the adjuster walk you through each stage of the qualification process and the basics about the policy.
- What types of care does the policy cover? For example, does it cover home health care and all levels of nursing home care? Is there a difference in coverage at home versus at a facility?
- Are there any specific requirements that home caregivers or a facility must meet for the coverage to apply?
- What documentation will the insurance company need to qualify your selected care? If the insurance company will not accept your proposed caregivers, all is not lost. Ask what type of experience might be acceptable.
- How long is the elimination period (waiting period)? This is the period that you must pay out of pocket before the insurance policy applies.
- Understand the insurance company's requirements for an assessment of your loved one. If there is an in-person assessment, ask the long-term

care insurance company if you can sit in on the assessment of your loved one's mental state.

- Understand the documentation required for reimbursement. What is the best way to submit the documentation to be paid in a timely manner? Can you pay your caregivers or an assisted living facility by wire transfer? Must fraud waivers be signed? How often? By whom?
- Is there a difference in premium for care in a facility versus care in the home?
- Does the process change if you are using an agency?
- When is your premium due? Does the premium change throughout the life of the policy, or does the premium remain the same during the policy life?
- Is renewal of the policy guaranteed if premiums are paid?
- When can the insurance company cancel the policy?
- Is there a second person on the policy that the insurance company will notify in case you miss the bill for the premium amount? Can you add someone?
- How does payment work? Do they pay a set amount per day? How long will payment continue? Is there a maximum benefit by amount or by time period?
- Is there an automatic adjustment for inflation?
- How long will it take the company to pay you after they receive the information?
- How often does your loved one need to be reassessed for coverage to continue? What does that reassessment consist of (in-person meeting, documentation only)?
- Does your coverage end after a certain number of years, or once a specific amount has been paid by the insurer?

Consider additional training for yourself.

The Alzheimer's Association offers free courses on a variety of topics through its Education Center, including legal and financial planning, understanding and responding to dementia related behavior, and tailored courses for each of the Early Stage, Middle Stage, and Late Stages of Alzheimer's dementia.[5] You may wish to take the essentiALZ®— Alzheimer's Association Training and Certification Course, even if you do not wish to take the certification test.[6] The course follows the Alzheimer's Association Dementia Care Practice Recommendations and provides students of the course with very helpful and important information about effective communication and care of people living with Alzheimer's. The AARP Home & Family Caregiving site is also a useful resource.[7] Understanding the disease and its effect on the brain, and learning techniques that a caregiver can use to diffuse frustrating situations and meaningfully engage with a loved one can greatly improve not only your experience, but also your loved one's experience.

Accept the fact that your loved one may reject help.

Unfortunately, there are no easy solutions to this scenario. Although your loved one's rejection of help is completely understandable, as the mere existence of help can mean one is no longer independent, becoming the parent of your own parent is incredibly difficult. Try not to internalize this rejection as a rejection of your good faith concern and efforts. Your loved one may not think he or she needs help. You may want to refer to the caregiver by another name, such as an "assistant" or a "helper." Start slow. This may be a recurring conversation. Perhaps a few hours a week at first to allow the caregivers to earn your loved one's trust. Identify tasks your loved one does not like to do and suggest that the "assistant" help with these tasks to free up time for more enjoyable pursuits. If there is a dementia day care in your area, ask for a tour or if you and your loved one can attend a class together for free. If your loved one likes art, perhaps you could try out an art class. If your loved one is mentally able and amenable, include them in the conversation. Consider the help of a third party, such as a trusted doctor or spiritual guide. Sometimes a third party can seem more objective than family, particularly the children of the person with Alzheimer's.

PORTULACA

By Jane P. Moreland

My mother leads me to a black iron plate,
my father's name in white slide letters.
She's ordered a headstone but can't decide
what words. Full name with no initials? Do I think
months, days, years or just years? She wants
no nicknames. But would I mind the last stanza
of a poem he liked, one I wrote when I was twelve,
in small letters around the border?

I look at the graves before him in this plot.
They're all here, the grandparents, aunts, and uncles,
old side of the table at family dinners,
as polished black granite, ivy
like heavy eyebrows over the edges,
every name and date spelled out. I vote the same
for my father, thinking of someday genealogists.
They'll want to know everything.

The grave is aflame in portulaca she's planted,
bronze-red like the casket, to fill the gaps
until the grass grows. She rearranges
fleshy stems to cover sand lumpy with settling
after a week of rain. Into a deep crack,
she thrusts her arm past the elbow, can't find him.
She's here every afternoon, she says. After years
of taking care, she can't seem to stop now.

The sun's sinking into red haze as we leave.
A breeze stirs lonely beards of moss
in oaks above as shadows close the portulaca,
and flush dark stones of others stain the shade.
From the car, I can't see my father's name,
only a bar in the grass, dark hyphen, like a mark
I'd leave where words stopped my heart
on a page I might come back to.

Chapter 7

Traveling with Your Alzheimer's Companion

Parents driving. They have driven us for decades, but at a point in time, their children believe that they should no longer drive. With my father, we negotiated a deal. He would take a driving test from a mutually agreed independent instructor. If he passed, I would drop the subject. If he failed, he would hand over the keys and never drive again. Of course, he passed. He used every bit of focus and grit to be the perfect driver during the thirty-minute test. I had underestimated his resolve. He passed the course, and a deal is a deal.

For my mother, the subject of driving was much more difficult. I do not think she even wanted to drive, but the thought of not being allowed to drive equated to losing independence. She had driven for decades. She had a perfect driving record except for an accident in her teenage years when fiddling with the radio. *How could her children dictate her driving privileges? What right did they have to make these decisions? What right do they have to tell her what she can and cannot do?* She was a perfect driver. Teenage years don't count! After all, she had taught us how to drive—*how can the student tell the teacher to surrender the keys?*

After a bit of coaxing, she seemed to be happy to allow Liz or Kathy to drive her around. We reminded her of the Houston traffic; "Isn't it just easier to let Liz and Kathy drive you? Less stressful." She eventually reluctantly agreed that Liz and Kathy could drive when they were at the house, but this was her choice. Taking the keys away was quite different. That was not her choice. That was her children unjustly forcing their incorrect views onto her. However, we were understandably concerned she might get in the car for an errand and get lost or have an accident.

The keys always hung on a key holder nailed to the wall across from the garage door. She looked for the keys—if the car keys were on her keyring hanging in its intended location, she was happy. If they had disappeared, she was angry and annoyed. She would walk by the door to the garage several times per day, checking to see if the car keys were there. Then, a lightbulb—*why not obtain a fake car key that looked exactly like her key, put it on her key ring, and hang it on the keyholder?* The real key would be in another location known only to us, Liz, and Kathy. Magic. It worked. I think all she wanted was the power to know she could drive if she wanted to drive—that the ability to choose to drive had not been taken away from her. Her children could force "friends" on her, but they could not take away the freedom of the car.

Once we realized the effect of the fake car key, we were liberated. A door opened to a new avenue of thought and strategy. *What else can we "fake car key?" Can we "fake car key" checks? Can we "fake car key" credit cards?* The "fake car key" ushered in an era of simultaneous independence and dependence. Perhaps fake car-keying makes me a hypocrite. On the one hand, I preach of telling your loved one the truth. On the other hand, we fake car-keyed many things in the name of safety. Well, so be it.

When I reflect on the times with my mother before her Alzheimer's, it's difficult to reconcile the mom of my youth with Baby Jane. Mom and I used to take little trips together—we drove together to my college in Virginia. We shared driving and stopped at interesting places. We listened to AM radio and talked politics. We stopped at outlet malls and shopped. As it was the age before cell phones and maps on phones or navigation devices, we were delighted and cheered at each turn of our AAA Trip Tick, a rectangular book that was a paper map of your journey.

I was constantly ill during my junior and senior year of college. I finally went to see a doctor in Charlottesville at the University of Virginia. "When in doubt, yank them out." He recommended removing my tonsils. The first call, of course, was to my mother. Despite my age of twenty, I was terrified about the operation. I had never undergone anesthesia. She offered to fly up and stay with me for as long as I needed. I remember laying in the recovery area in my after-surgery haze listening to my mother quite insistently asking very specific questions about my surgery. She had clearly read up on tonsils. I drifted off to sleep knowing that Mom was on the case. She was the most capable person I knew. I felt safe.

After college, when I lived in New York, Mom would visit me occasionally for long weekends. I would buy tickets for shows and stay with her at her hotel. I relished the thought of an elevator rather than my five-floor walkup. I could only afford the worst seats, but she was always happy. I would take her to my favorite outdoor markets. I showed her the thrift shops I frequented. We visited museums. Sometimes, we would just walk and enjoy the city. We would enjoy a long brunch and chat about nothing, just like we did at home in Houston. She would order room service breakfast. Occasionally she would meet me for lunch downtown during my lunch break. She always encouraged me to try my best, and despite my desire to fake illness and skip work to play with her, she insisted that I fulfill my work commitments.

We traveled to New Orleans. We walked along Royal Street. We saw paintings of the Blue Dog and the Red Cat. We talked about why people liked those paintings and speculated about the next animal that might find fame. We ate turtle soup au sherry at the Court of Two Sisters. We visited antique shops along Magazine Street. We enjoyed the tourist attractions of the French Market. We never ate beignets at Café Du Monde—too fattening, not nutritious. Sometimes she could be a real downer.

We traveled to San Antonio and ate steak at a restaurant on the Riverwalk. We covered our outfits with heavy wool ponchos provided by the restaurant due to the cold weather. We enjoyed looking at the people and boats passing by. Although neither of us drank coffee in the evening, we each ordered decaf coffees after our meal because neither of us wanted to leave.

Before I started law school in New Orleans, my mother helped me find an apartment. She gave me old furniture from the attic and taught me how to refinish it. She offered thoughtful suggestions even though she was not a lawyer. She and Dad frequently visited during law school. They always stayed at the Pontchartrain Hotel in the Richard Burton Suite. Now, that room no longer exists, nor do they.

Shortly after Dad died, my mother and I traveled to Virginia. It was difficult. Changing planes in Charlotte was difficult, but doable. I allowed for double the amount of time normally required to check in and walk to the gate. I wanted us to be able to walk slowly and experience little stress. We checked all our luggage so we would not need to carry it. I investigated whether there was an airline club we could stop into during the layover. I think those are always much calmer. Less hustle and bustle. Mom walked slowly, but with a smile on her face. We laughed about the gate numbers—so funny-sounding, A1, B10, A5. We counted together as we approached our gate. I repeatedly reminded her of our gate number. I offered to oversee and keep all documentation and crowned myself the Queen of Documentation. She laughed and agreed that might be a good idea. She remarked that all the walking was good exercise.

Balancing the inevitable conference calls and Mom during our trip was stressful. I was always afraid she would wander away, be afraid, feel lost, or become lonely and forget why she was sitting where I had asked her to sit. That never happened during our trip, however. She stayed exactly where I asked. We had a lovely time together. We went to restaurants during the day, enjoyed afternoon tea, and walked in nature on easy and short trails. She was confused, of course, but she knew my name and that I was her daughter. This time has passed. Once it passes, it is gone forever. How I wish I could return to that time and tell her how much I love her, although I tell myself that she felt my love.

Later during her disease, we drove to the beach at Bolivar Peninsula, where her sister lived, to eat lunch. My sons sat in the back seat, and Mom sat in the front passenger seat. She sat silently during the ride, watching the road ahead. Occasionally, I would try to start a conversation, which was met with one-word responses or short sentences. She asked me several times during the drive where we were going. My aunt had thoughtfully prepared an activity before lunch. We made necklaces using seashells my aunt had collected, beads and other odds and ends. Having an activity was a wonderful idea. My sons and I sat at the table with Mom making necklaces. It is a day I will always remember fondly.

As the Alzheimer's disease progressed, travel became more and more difficult. There was a long period of time when I could explain to her how to get into the front seat of the car. I would fasten her seatbelt like a small child, and we would be on our way. However, that ability eventually waned, and transport by wheelchair in a special van was the only viable option. At the very end of her life, she returned to her nursing home by ambulance in a stretcher, as she was having trouble holding herself up in a seated position. As Kathy once told me, we are once an adult, but twice a baby.

Driving and Alzheimer's Disease

There will come a time when someone living with Alzheimer's should not be driving, for their own safety and for the safety of the people around them. Look for signs that the person should stop driving, such as:

- Accidents, scratches, or dents on the car or surrounding areas, such as the garage. Evaluate your loved one's driving ability after any incident.
- Difficulty remembering directions to frequently visited locations.
- Indications that the person may have gotten lost, such as taking a long time to run a routine errand without a reasonable explanation.
- Increased traffic tickets.
- Comments from other people who have either ridden with the individual as a passenger or observed unsafe driving.
- Hazardous driving—speeding, changing lanes suddenly, forgetting to use a blinker, failing to stop at traffic lights or stop signs, and forgetting which pedal is the gas and which is the brake are all examples of hazardous driving.

- Doctor recommendations to change driving habits.
- Hearing, mobility, or vision changed that may affect one's ability to drive safely.[1]

The laws of certain states, such as California, require physicians to report an individual's Alzheimer's diagnosis to the state's health department or department of motor vehicles.[2] However, this type of mandatory reporting requirement does not exist in most states.[3] Therefore, most of us are left to devise strategies to ensure our loved one stops driving. Below is a list of strategies to consider.

- Discuss your concerns openly and in a loving manner with your loved one.
- Take the individual to get a driving test, stating that it is necessary for a new driver's license.
- Discuss your concerns with the individual's physician. Explain the reasons you believe the individual should stop driving. Note hazardous driving you have witnessed. Ask the physician to tell the individual to stop driving. Perhaps the physician can write a prescription on a prescription pad, such as "Do Not Drive." You and/or the physician can show the prescription to your loved one.
- Ask the individual's physician to refer the loved one for a driver evaluation program. The American Occupational Therapy Association offers such evaluation programs. The intent of the program is to assess whether an individual can continue to drive safely. These evaluation programs may or may not require a doctor's referral.
- Disconnect the car battery, invest in an auto-disabling device, or remove the distributor cap and explain that the individual cannot drive, because the car needs to be fixed.
- Move the car to another location and explain that the car is in the shop being serviced.
- Hide the car keys.[4]

Whether these strategies will work is highly dependent upon the individual. For example, in the case of my mother, hiding car keys led to frustration, anger, and endless searches for car keys. She knew we had hidden the keys from her, which eroded trust. Although she was sympathetic to our open and loving conversations, they were not effective, because she believed her children were wrong. In our case, the façade of choice through the fake car key did the trick. Once you find a strategy that works, you might be able to utilize your new strategy in other situations.

Travel Tips

For someone living with Alzheimer's, traveling is extremely disruptive, as it is a complete change of routine. Whether it is advisable for your loved one to travel will depend upon the stage of Alzheimer's and your specific situation. However, here are some tips and resources if you decide to take a trip.

- Plan. What is the least disruptive mode of travel?
- Travel during the daytime. Traveling during the daytime is advisable because many people living with Alzheimer's become agitated later in the day.
- Check your main bags. Checking bags is helpful because keeping an eye on your loved one will be difficult if you are also managing a lot of luggage.
- Ideally, travel with one other person in addition to your loved one. Traveling with a companion in addition to someone living with Alzheimer's will allow you to take breaks. If one person needs to go to the restroom or relax for a minute, the other person can be with your loved one to make sure he or she does not wander. Another person will provide you with someone to talk to so that you do not feel lonely or sad.
- Inform airport security that you are traveling with someone living with Alzheimer's and have your loved one go through airport security before you. If you are behind your loved one, you can

watch and intervene if they have issues with security. If you are in front of your loved one, they might get confused and wander away from the airport security line.

- Make sure your loved one has identifying information on him or her, such as an identifying bracelet, necklace, or a clothing tag. A sheet with contact details in your loved one's pocket might work too.
- Conduct research about where you might rest during a layover at the airport. Is there a restaurant where you might sit at a table? Is there an airline club?
- Allow for double the amount of time when you travel by air. This extra time will avoid a lot of stress.
- Call the airline and arrange for a transport to your next gate or to baggage claim. Inform them that you are traveling with someone diagnosed with Alzheimer's.
- Make sure you have all your loved one's important documentation with you, such as the medical power of attorney, as well as important medications. Put these in your carry-on bag. Keep a picture on your phone.
- Assume responsibility for boarding passes and important documentation for the trip. If your loved one refuses, print off or have in your phone an extra copy. This way, if the document is lost, it's OK.
- Take snacks with you. Airport food is expensive and purchasing snacks will require you to take your eyes off your loved one. If you are driving, having a snack handy might eliminate a stop along the way. A snack is also a fun diversion.
- Listen to soothing music for its calming effect.
- Taking a travel game, a fidget tool or fidget blanket, a stress ball, or another sensory object might be soothing and provide a needed distraction. Some people living with Alzheimer's enjoy having on their lap a doll or a small toy pet.
- Recognize that your trip will be different than past trips.

Celebrate the activities your loved one can still do, recognizing that activities you used to enjoy may not be feasible. Simple activities like a short walk, a cup of tea, a quiet meal, or a simple board game can be comforting and fun. Try to avoid overstimulating activities for your loved one.

- The Alzheimer's Association provides several travel tips on their website, including information about a wandering support service that will reconnect you with your loved one if he or she has wandered and assist with medical emergencies.[5]

THRIFT

By Jane P. Moreland

They ask why I speak
when you can't hear me,
why I stay since even if you see
you won't remember. I should leave
for fresh air. In your rarefied sky,
you won't miss me.

Waste Not, Want Not
is where it comes from, my grandmother's
cross-stitch sampler, code that raised me.
Bake with sour milk. Plait strips
of outgrown skirts into rugs.
Save coins in secret jars. Don't waste
one precious drop of you.

Chapter 8

Maximizing the Quality of Life

When Mom started to need twenty-four-hour care, life became even more challenging. We were fortunate to have wonderful private caregivers, but people need vacations, become ill, or have family emergencies. I supplemented with an agency; however, once you start depending upon an agency it's a new world. There are a lot of unknowns. *Will someone show up? Who will show up? Will the person be someone Mom has not met? Will he or she interact with Mom or just watch TV all day? What if Mom takes a walk and gets lost? What if someone stops by the house and takes advantage of her?* I dated a man once whose mother was sold a $5,000 vacuum by a door-to-door salesman. Twenty-four-hour care is also incredibly expensive.

Mom was not used to the agency people and found certain things to be annoying. There was one woman who ate nuts very loudly. Mom would repeatedly tell me how loudly she ate her nuts. She could hear nut crunching rooms away. I did not believe her until I stopped by to validate the cacophony of nut crunching. She was right. It was like her mouth was some type of echo chamber or she was sending out echo-location signals to mark her location. A human bat. We made a "no nuts at work" rule. It was a superbly uncomfortable conversation about nuts, nut sounds, types of nuts, and associated sounds. Just a straight rule, thank you. No more nuts at work. Not even the softer ones like cashews.

Another day I stopped by on the weekend to see that the living room couch had been made up like a bed. Mom had spent the night on the couch and not in her bedroom. She had become confused in the night and wet the couch. Of course, she did. The couch smelled like urine. She was also very sore from sleeping on the couch and more confused than normal. The agency caregiver said she thought sleeping on the couch would be better for my mother. *What? When is it ever more comfortable to sleep on a couch than in your own bedroom?* It just made no sense.

At this point, my mother was still able to dress herself and go to the bathroom independently. She needed help with bathing. She walked at a slower pace and much more carefully, but no cane or walker was needed. I recall we attended a talk at the refurbished Julia Ideson Library in downtown Houston. She found the shiny tile floor very unsettling and walked slowly, fearing she would fall. She ate independently, but like with many things, she required prompts or reminders.

I had become increasingly concerned about my mother's diet in terms of its nutritional value and variety. Since there was no longer cooking, her meals generally consisted of microwavable items, sandwiches, and fruits. Consequently, we began making her favorite recipes at my house and delivering them to her in storage containers. Although she loved these mouthfuls of memories, this solution was not sustainable.

My children and I took a summer vacation with our dear friends to a place called Moody Gardens, which is about an hour from Houston. As I sat on a bench watching my children traverse a multilevel ropes course, I spoke with Mom's primary care physician and explained all these concerns, as well as the struggles I was experiencing keeping all the balls in the air. After a long discussion, he gently suggested the idea of assisted living at a nursing home. I simultaneously felt relief and guilt. Relief because many of these challenges would be resolved. Her diet would improve. She would have more social interaction and possibly new friends. She would attend classes, which I thought she would find enjoyable. I would no longer need to maintain contingency plans if I needed to skip work and take care of Mom. The risk of wandering would be greatly reduced. Guilt because my mother would leave her beloved home of forty years. Guilt that being placed in a new environment might accelerate her decline. Guilt because the move to a facility would improve my life, but possibly make her life worse. Guilt that I felt relief. Guilt that I believed my father would not have approved. To this day, I feel guilt, a useless and pointless emotion that trespasses into my heart and mind, even though I know in retrospect that being in a facility greatly improved her quality of life.

After the discussion with Mom's doctor, the next step was socializing the idea of a move with family and making sure everyone was on the same page. While I looked into insurance coverage and cost of care, another relative agreed to make a "short list" of possible locations. Once there was a short list, we contacted the facilities for tours. After much discussion, we decided to move her to a facility. We leased a room and got everything ready for Mom to seamlessly move into her new home.

Mom would initially live on an assisted living floor. She would have an itinerary of classes, go to outings with groups, and eat downstairs in the restaurant. After her Alzheimer's progressed, she would move to a memory care floor in the same building, which afforded a higher standard of care.

We talked to the facility about how to manage the move. How would Mom feel about being in a different place? She had lived in her house for over forty years. *How would she feel about missing furniture that we moved to her new room while getting it ready?* She would no longer have a backyard. The facility suggested replacing empty spots where furniture had been moved with other furniture of a similar size. She will notice a large space, but she may not notice a change in furniture or different items on the wall.

After Mom left for a long lunch and afternoon visit with a relative, we got to work. There was a painting over the fireplace of a former family home in Galveston, Texas, that had been in the same location for decades. It was directly across from her usual place on the couch. We moved this painting to her new home and replaced it with a similarly sized wall hanging from a different room. We moved a coffee table in front of the couch to the nursing facility and replaced it with a small bamboo table from another part of the house. A relic from my father's college days. It was completely out of place. We took her framed photographs of grandchildren from the coffee table and replaced them with other trinkets. Chairs were replaced with other chairs of different colors. The salmon-colored chair next to the living room couch was replaced with a blue chair. We did not mention the changes, waiting for her reaction. To our amazement, she noticed nothing. She seamlessly moved into her new home. It was a surprisingly easy transition.

At her new home, there was a restaurant with decent food, activities, and friends. For a while, my mother had a vibrant social life. She loved the classes. She laughed with friends. She was engaged. Occasionally, she would watch the movie after dinner. Her room was full of her favorite possessions and pictures of her loved ones. She was always happy to see me until the final stages of her disease—even if I was "That Nice Lady." "You are just such a nice lady!" "There is that nice lady!" "I like you, Nice Lady!" At some point I stopped explaining that I was her daughter. Just being The Nice Lady was okay with me, and honestly, by that time I don't think she understood the concept of a "daughter."

By the date of my mother's death, I had been born and re-born multiple times. She was always so happy to see me, even if she had no idea who I was. When I saw her at the nursing home I would say, "Hello, Mom. It's me, your daughter, Mary." "Why Jane, I did not know you had a daughter!" "Why didn't you tell me?" her friends would say. With smiles of joy, she would exclaim with a broad smile, "I didn't know!"

"The good news is that you do have a daughter. I am your daughter, and I am happy to see you." She was so happy. The Nice Lady was her daughter. A celebration. It was bittersweet every time. Everyone smiled and laughed. I fought back tears but pretended to be delighted. I was the middle-aged Nice Lady who had just been born. Welcome to life, Nice Lady.

One day I visited her, and I remember for a moment, just wanting to stay. Just wanting to stay in her room—a girl and her mom. I don't think she remembered her lovely house, but she remembered me. Maybe not my name exactly, but she knew I was one of her people. In fact, I was "The Nice Lady." The Nice Lady was an amazing and cool person! Everyone loved The Nice Lady. In my mind I briefly fantasized about just moving in—no cooking, cleaning, no laundry, no monitoring of electronic devices, no thorny legal problems. Just me and Mom. Laughing about nothing. We could even watch the Hallmark channel Jane liked, but that bored my mother.

In my fantasy, we would go to classes. "The birds and the_____?" the teacher would ask. "Bees!!!" we would both yell out simultaneously with smiles and great satisfaction. "Jimmy crack corn and I don't_____?" "CARE!!!" we would scream in delight. We would copy the Xerox picture of a duck with our own watercolors side by side. We would choose different colors and comment to each other on the beauty of our ducks. We would visit the garden outside and look at the birds. We would eat at the restaurant and order dessert. Swimming noodles would be magically transformed into weights for our exercise class only to later turn into baseball bats for the big game.

Sure, this was not like some of our other trips. Not New York. Not Hot Springs. Not San Antonio. Not New Orleans. It was a different type of trip—still fun. However, although Jane's life was fading away, my life continued. My children needed me, and I needed them. The babysitter wanted to go home. It was time to say goodbye.

Even though Mom's wardrobe changed, she still loved clothing. My mother always purchased black shoes because they were practical, stylish, and went well with her black pants. Jane's eyes would light up at a pair of red shoes. Occasionally, I would match scarves with shirts in her closet and place the scarf on the hanger with the shirt. She always liked a silk scarf. One time I arrived on the fifth floor, and almost all the ladies were wearing scarves. *Can you say fashion trend?* All these wardrobe and other changes are stressful and painful. I wish I could say they were not. Just focus on what your loved one needs—forget the heels of old, the skinny black flats, and the tailored jacket with a pencil skirt. While the dress code has changed, your loved one can still look dignified and feel great.

People tell me what a great daughter I was, how lucky Jane was to have me. Despite these kind words, I still feel guilty about not visiting more, not doing more. I know these feelings are not helpful. I know my mother knew that I loved her very much. However, each time I saw a child taking care of a mom with a perfectly organized closet, superb outfit and matching shoes, my heart sank a bit. That mom had it better. But the fact that my mother did not have an organized closet or ran out of stool softener or shampoo on a Sunday evening did not mean I loved her any less than family members of those with perfectly stocked closets and bathrooms.

A primary caregiver of a person living with Alzheimer's is always on call in case something occurs. Being in the sandwich generation means that calls can come from all sides—the school, the father, the companion, the nursing home, the doctor—and at all hours. Even if your young children are safe and with you, your Alzheimer's mother could be in distress. Flexibility is key. Have a ready list of relatives, neighbors, friends, and babysitters who might assist is a necessity. Not everyone has this list. I suggest going to an Alzheimer's or dementia support meeting close to your home and trying to find a network. Ask parents of your children's friends if they know of anyone taking care of older relatives. Create a network. Suggest the idea. Once you get the word out, you might be surprised by how many people are in a similar situation. At a minimum, the network will hopefully provide you with new friends.

I was always concerned about something happening to me. Family members would take over in my absence, of course, but I worried about the inevitable transition period. I also traveled internationally quite frequently for work. Receiving a call about your mom needing a doctor's visit or supplies while you are in a foreign country is stressful. My children were young, and I was uncomfortable with them staying in the house alone. So, when the call came that Mom needed something or was ill, I either had to drag my children along or make other arrangements for my boys quickly. With private caregivers, this is much easier to manage. With a private caregiver, you have another adult with whom you can tag-team. Once Mom moved to a facility, this became much more difficult. With small children, an emergency trip on a Sunday evening to see a doctor is not an easy task. Just asking for the help is excruciating. Asking for help means you must explain.

Therefore, I had a personal goal of putting Mom on autopilot. I was afraid something would happen to me, and she would be lost. Her medications should refill and be delivered automatically. Some pharmacies will deliver for free. Her personal items, such as underwear, toothpaste, soap, and shampoo, should also be delivered. For a while, I tried Amazon subscriptions—goods were delivered at regular intervals. However, items were often lost between the delivery door and Mom's room. I spent several weekends trying to locate our supplies in the mailroom of her facility. Later, I located a small family-owned business that visited residents of the nursing home and supplied whatever they needed in terms of personal care. The company took inventory of supplies. This was very helpful, as sometimes I suspected Mom's supplies were being used for others who had run out and, knowing that I was challenged at keeping things well stocked, I imagine other residents assisted Mom from time to time. Once inventory began, I felt like the purchases of supplies became less erratic and much more predictable in terms of cost, which made planning much easier.

Sundowning is a real thing. Some individuals living with Alzheimer's become very angry, yell, hit, even throw things late in the day. When my mother moved to the memory care floor, I eventually stopped visiting her in the evenings. It was startling seeing people who were normally so calm during the day turn into angry, yelling beings a few short hours later. It was distressing, and I felt like I was in the way. However, occasionally, my mother would need something late in the day, and I found myself in the middle of sundowning time.

Carolyn was a young person on the floor. I never quite understood her illness. However, for an unknown reason, I could almost always make Carolyn laugh. We had a connection. She stuttered quite a bit and struggled to articulate her thoughts. Typically, I would just repeat what she said back to me, agreed to it, and smiled. Simple techniques that required patience, but they always worked. I always was happy to see Carolyn. "Hello, Carolyn. You are looking wonderful today!" She would smile and say hello back. However, one day, while we were sitting calmly together at a table watching TV, Carolyn's eyes bored intensely into me, and she started yelling directly at me for no reason whatsoever. I got butterflies in my stomach—in a bad way. I was a bit scared. I was so shocked I froze. An employee, called a "Pal" at the facility, fortunately intervened and diffused the situation.

There was a woman on the fifth floor who was so happy normally, but occasionally, she wanted to leave. "Why did they lock me in here?" "How could my children have done this to me?" she would yell. On a certain level, she was correct. She literally was locked in. I am sure this would have broken her children's hearts.

There was a son at the nursing home who visited his mother quite often. He took her out to lunch frequently. He visited her on the fifth floor and ate meals with the residents. He was the most attentive son. Sometimes they would leave for the day, and he would return her to the fifth floor, kiss her on the cheek, tell her he loved her, and leave. Five minutes later, his mother might ask why her son never visited her. She was upset, angry. "Why doesn't he visit me?"

A gentleman after dinner one day started throwing his glasses and plates. The Pals quickly isolated the gentleman and moved everyone one else out of the way. My mother looked at me, laughed, and said, "What is his problem?"

There was a period when my mother became aggressive. The details are difficult to write. I was told that she tried to bite someone. She yelled. She hit. She was mean. Flashbacks filled my brain to discussions with other parents about toddlers who had bitten other toddlers. I spoke with her doctor who put her on anti-psychotic medication. It was a sobering and sad realization. Obviously, the disease had progressed. Her mind had changed. However, the medication was necessary. I was so relieved and felt very fortunate that she returned to her relaxed and happy self.

The nursing home was always thinking of new ways to entertain their residents and honor their lives. One day, Mom was "highlighted." I was invited to speak at the event about Mom's life and accomplishments. My mother was a talented poet. At the last minute I thought—oh, I will read a poem as part of my talk. I was busy with life and running late, so I just located and printed the first one I could find on the internet before leaving my office without really giving it much thought. It was titled "Prunings." The poem was poignant. The residents listened politely with blank stares. The shocked facial expressions of the employees reacting to the poem was priceless. Jane was amazed and pleasantly surprised to learn that she was a published author, whatever that meant! She also enjoyed making funny sounds in the microphone and then laughing hysterically. It was a sad, yet somehow hilarious, afternoon.

PRUNINGS

By Jane P. Moreland
(published in Poetry, June 1982)

1

Cherry Laurels of a certain age
thicken at branch ends, shade out leaves
between ends and trunk. Branches sag
from their natural curves. So you prune,
cutting back limbs, shaping bare cones that look dreadful.
The neighbors know the trees are dead.
But you know that even before you've tied cuttings,
signals have reached root filaments,
and that after roots expand enough,
dormant buds will break from bark,
the skeleton fleshing out as the trunk extends,
top growth seeking balance with its roots.

2

Your mother drops by on Saturdays
between florist and jelly doughnuts
on her rounds bringing suggestions:
don't lend your brother a dime,
don't have any more children,
invite Uncle Carl to Easter.
Most days you try not to listen and answer,
but today you hear, reply as sharply
as if your tongue were yellow-handled ratchet shears:
that's between you and your brother,
you'll have as many children as you please,
you wouldn't have that bastard in your house.
She jerks up straight, eyes startled,
her face pale as she departs.
Do not take her silence for silence.

Maximizing the Quality of Life

Routines bring stability and comfort.
A person living with Alzheimer's has trouble understanding new information. A consistent routine decreases the stress of the caregiver and reduces the anxiety of the individual. Knowing the schedule for the day and practicing activities on a regular basis can increase self-esteem. You can write the schedule on a calendar or a whiteboard posted on the wall.

Devise a strategy for "sundowning."
Sundowning is a term referring to circumstances of increased confusion, disorientation, anxiety, or agitation beginning late in the day and continuing during the evening. People living with Alzheimer's who experience sundowning may pace back and forth, yell, have extreme mood swings, refuse to follow directions, wander, become aggressive, and even throw things.[1] If observing sundowning is an emotional, distressing, or unmanageable experience for you, you will want to locate additional assistance late in the day and evening or—if your loved one is in a nursing home—avoid visiting during these times. At the nursing home where my mother lived, I noticed they closed all curtains in the afternoon, so that the residents could not notice the change in outside light. They also included walks during the day and minimized evening activities. Here is a list of tips that may help caregivers manage sundowning:

- Rest is important. The more well-rested you are, the less likely you are to perform unintended, nonverbal behavior that will aggravate sundowning. You will also be able to more easily empathize with your loved one and put sundowning in perspective.
- Mornings are best for those who live with dementia. Scheduling activities such as baths and doctor appointments in the morning when your loved one is more alert can ease the process.

- Routines bring comfort. Implement a regular routine throughout the day that includes activities the person enjoys. Fresh air and sunlight are also important. Within daily activities, provide room for time outside (weather permitting, of course!).
- Be a detective. Track what activities happen before a sundowning event so that you can identify triggers to sundowning. This will help you be better prepared for later occurrences. It may also help you alter the person's schedule to help ease the effects of sundowning.
- Make notes of what activities calm your loved one. Keep this list on hand when the individual becomes agitated or stressed. Examples of calming activities are listening to calming music or sounds of nature (such as the sounds of the beach or rainstorms), reviewing photo albums, and holding a toy pet or doll.
- Stimulation in the late hours can increase confusion and agitation. Minimize activities such as playing loud music, watching TV, and doing chores to reduce chances of stress.
- Take advantage of larger lunches and smaller dinners.
- Make sure your home or space where the person is staying is well-lit. This can reduce confusion. Close the curtains or blinds.
- Avoid physical restraints whenever possible. Hindering movements will increase stress. The individual will also not understand why they are being restrained, which will increase agitation and confusion.
- Let the person pace back and forth with supervision, or take a walk with the individual. Both activities reduce restlessness.
- Consult with your physician to understand what times of day work best for your loved one's medication.[2]

The above suggestions consist of changes to a person's environment and behaviors; however, these may not work. When these changes are not effective, talk to your loved one's physician about the situation to see if there are medications or other strategies to try.[3]

Empathize with your loved one.

Your feelings will be hurt when your loved one forgets your name, becomes angry, or says something ugly. You will frequently feel loss and sadness. A rebuffed hug should not be taken personally. Try to empathize with your loved one's point of view. Your loved one may not recognize who you are, and as painful as this is to accept, your hug is that of a stranger. How would you feel if someone you did not know tried to grab you? This is the disease, not you. You may have to continuously remind yourself of that fact.

Take care of yourself, physically and mentally.

Take care of your physical health by eating well, exercising, and going to the doctor. Don't forget about your mental health. Talk to a counselor if that would be helpful. Locate friends or acquaintances with Alzheimer's experience. Reach out to the Alzheimer's Association or a nearby church and join a support group. Make a list of things that you like to do. Accept that if you have focused intensely on your career and children up to this date, you may no longer have any hobbies. If you have nothing for your list, make a list of one or two realistic hobbies that you would like to try. The internet is a game-changer for hobbies. Music lessons can be taken at your computer. You can connect with a live language tutor in another country through a computer. If you sit in front of a computer all day, you may wish to try gardening or cooking, which are activities you can do at home. Schedule "me time." Resist the urge to have your regular "fun activity" be a glass of Chardonnay or a cocktail, which can be a slippery slope. Plan to call someone for lunch, dinner, or a movie once a month. If you are too busy to leave the house, perhaps a video call with a friend on a regular basis might help. Find and plan something healthy that you can look forward to on a regular basis. There are many outlets where you can go for ideas and assistance.[4]

Brainstorm about what you can put on "auto-pilot."
For example, mail order pharmacies or local pharmacies with auto refill can take a task off your to-do list. Some local pharmacies will deliver for free. If your loved one is in assisted living, the facility likely has an existing relationship with a pharmacy. Consider having supplies, such as underwear, lotion, toothpaste, and shampoo delivered at regular intervals through a subscription.

Take advantage of telehealth and mobile services.
Traveling to see the dentist or a doctor can be a difficult experience both for you and your loved one. To the extent possible, take advantage of telehealth doctor's visits and mobile dentists that you can arrange at regular intervals. Health insurance or Medicare might cover quarterly dentist cleaning visits, and quarterly visits will help to avoid cavities.

Consider hospice care.
Hospice care is a type of medical care for people at the final stages of illness. Prior to putting my mother in hospice, I understood that hospice care was intended only when death is imminent. However, this is not correct; people living with late-stage Alzheimer's can qualify for hospice care. Hospice allowed my mother to receive additional care, and the hospice nurse and case manager checked on her regularly. They were also an excellent resource about what might happen next and provided thoughtful ideas for improving Mom's standard of living.

Tips for Maximizing Quality of Life

Early/Middle Stages
- Telephones you can program with pictures of individuals on speed dial, rather than numbers, are helpful. Your loved one does not

need to manage locating the number and putting it into the phone.

- Pictures with labels of names of people in large font are helpful reminders of who people are. There are also talking photo albums that allow you to record an explanation of each photo.
- Clocks with very large numbers that state the days of the week.
- A large print calendar to hang on the wall with lots of space for notes and appointments.
- A one-button radio or music box that is easy to operate.
- An automatic pill dispenser with an alarm.
- Appliance-use monitors, which allow you to monitor certain electrical devices at your loved one's home.
- A medical alert button.
- A nice smelling air freshener or fake flowers are inexpensive ways to make a room cheery.
- A whiteboard is excellent for notes, reminders, and kind notes from visitors.
- If reading is important to your loved one, consider a subscription to a magazine. *Mirador Magazine* was created specifically for people with cognitive impairment, such as people living with Alzheimer's. The magazine includes brief stories in short sentences and large font. There are also other fun features, such as puzzles and activities. The magazine is ad-free and visually quite attractive.[5]

Middle/Late Stages

- A GPS tracking device to assist you in locating your loved one in the event of wandering or getting lost.
- In-home video monitors.
- A fidget blanket or other type of sensory activity board.
- A stuffed animal or pet. You can purchase a "therapy" doll or pet that purrs or plays music.
- Large print books or coloring books.
- Costume jewelry.

- Pads for the bed in case of urine. More absorbent evening underwear or inserting an absorbent pad during nighttime. This will hopefully cut down on changing the sheets.
- An elevated toiled seat.
- In terms of room furniture, less is more. Your loved one will need plenty of room to move around.
- A walker with a seat makes frequent rest stops easier. You never have to find a chair!
- A VELCRO® Brand bag that fits on a walker or wheelchair to put things in.
- A wheelchair with a high back is helpful if your loved one has trouble sitting up.
- A blanket or a wheelchair blanket.
- A bed with an adjustable base will help your loved one get in and out of bed more easily. Invest in a decent mattress and a cozy blanket.
- If your loved one grips his or her hands, give them something to grip, such as a rolled-up hand towel.

The wardrobe may have changed, but your loved one can still look dignified:

- When purchasing clothing, consider whether it will be easy for someone to take on and off. Think about ease of use—a zipper might be easier than buttons. VELCRO® Brand products are easier than most things. Sports bras in a larger size that can slip over one's head are easier to put on and off than a traditional bra. Say goodbye to the lacey confidence-building lingerie of the past. Say hello to helping your mother into her oversized over-the-head brassiere.
- Iron-on nametags for clothing help your clothes not end up in a neighbor's room.
- Simple outfits are best. Monochrome outfits and solid color shirts always look dignified. Elastic waistband pants are comfortable. You can still look elegant with black or khaki pants and a solid shirt.

- Arrange the closet so that everything can be easily seen. Remove clothing from the closet that will not be worn or no longer fits. Rather than putting items in drawers, try to think of ways you can have them out in the open. For example, you can utilize transparent containers that you label "socks" or "underwear."
- Feet swell. Diabetic shoes with VELCRO® Brand closures and stretchy diabetic socks might be more comfortable. Maybe not the stylish black flats and trouser socks of old, but better for the occasion. Extra wide shoes are also an option.
- Cardigan sweaters, a poncho, or light jackets. My mother was always cold.

On Your Astonishment

By Jane P. Moreland

Again, you shock at events: your sister gone mad.
How did it happen?
Why weren't you warned?
There were signals: hairline crazings in porcelain glaze,
the first wet seepings, deepening fissures,
then nothing held back.
Nothing is constant. Things exist in transition
like the tides. Plums in a bowl rot from the seed out.
There are signs.

You see life in stills, glossy prints on black album pages,
sequences viewed in your haste as singular frames:
a smile, a rose, one wave and then another.

You miss the slow shrivels, the gradual swells,
the flushings and fadings, shading of petals from scarlet to garnet
before stem and calyx stand bare.

Nothing warns you. You see your mother's face,
miss her smile's stiffening, the slow graying of her flesh.
You see open water, not green's gradations
as the sea floor falls below reefs.

Chapter 9

Accepting the Inevitable— The Alzheimer's Descent

Not only is the disease cruel, but so is its progression. When Mom still lived at home, she and her caregiver would come over on the weekends, and we would all spend the day together. When she moved to a nursing home, I used to pick Mom up on the weekends and bring her to my house to spend the day with us. She laughed at the dogs. She watched her grandchildren and smiled. She was calm and content. We always had a good time, until one day we did not. Jane didn't want to be there. Jane felt uncomfortable. Jane said it was time for her to leave. She wanted to leave. She did not want to watch her grandsons or chat with me. She wanted nothing to eat. So, I sadly returned her to her new life.

Mom used to come to all school events. She loved them, even if she had no idea what was going on in the school play. Until one day, Jane became upset after going to a play in the packed middle school auditorium. Descending the stairs to our seats was difficult. It was dark. The clapping was loud. People she did not recognize greeted her warmly. It was heartbreaking to watch. Jane wanted to leave. "I think it is time for me to go home," she said. We found a quiet peaceful bench outside away from people while a friend fetched our car. She was happier on the bench, but still anxious and desperately wanted to leave and return to where she felt comfortable.

From that time forward, we just visited at her nursing home. She was at peace staying there. Shortly thereafter, the nursing home suggested moving Mom to the dreaded memory care floor, a floor with a charming name where you needed a code to unlock the door to enter and exit. The dreaded fifth floor. Meals were no longer served at the cheery restaurant downstairs with jazz music in the background, but instead in a large open room with tables, a sink, a refrigerator, and a dishwasher. Activities also took place on the fifth floor with occasional trips to the fourth floor, also a memory care floor. It was a life generally confined to a handful of rooms and hallways.

Mom would still smile at me when I entered the room. We still took classes together from time to time, but the classes were simpler. We enjoyed exercise classes using swimming noodles as weights. There was no longer bingo, but there were other games appropriate to the stage of the disease. Sometimes, we would just find a quiet couch and sit. Even on the memory care floor Mom laughed at silly things. Once when I visited, the residents were watching a movie—in Spanish. No one noticed. I said, "Hey, Mom, are you working on your Spanish?" She just laughed and laughed. She had not realized the movie was in Spanish. The Pal was embarrassed. Please, don't change it! Mom has always wanted to learn Spanish! Her daughter-in-law is from Spain! It was sad, but she was still there at some level—we laughed. I look at older pictures at my house during holidays, and she is laughing. I want my laughing mom.

My mother visited the same dental office for decades. She brushed and flossed her teeth every day, and unlike me, never feared a trip to have her teeth cleaned. On the contrary, she looked forward to it. She frequently reminded me of the correlation between dental care and lower risk of heart disease. However, as the disease progressed, she no longer understood why she was sitting in such an odd chair or what the dental hygienist was doing. She would not open her mouth. She did not recognize the receptionist she had known for decades and wanted to leave the office and walk out into the street because she did not belong there. When I tried to schedule her next appointment, the office informed me that they did not wish to continue treating my mother. They wished us the best. After several months of no visits to the dentist and calling around for a solution, I located a mobile dentist accustomed to treating persons living with Alzheimer's. After the first dental visit, they texted me a picture of my clearly confused but smiling mother holding a toiletry bag and wrapped in a blanket, both with their logo.

An assisted care facility is like a bubble. No one cares that you might forget what you desired to order for lunch. Maybe you can't even read the menu anymore—who cares! Food is food. If you are in a wheelchair, so are many others. Doorways are wide. Tables are far apart from each other. Feel free to stare out the window at nothing if you like. A simple "hi" is sufficient; don't even worry about remembering a name. It's all normal. Socks need not match. Schedules are approximations.

However, there comes a time when you must venture into the real world, and you realize your loved one has slipped more than you have realized. You have become used to being in the bubble, and the harsh reality of "normal" shows its ugly face.

For me, this moment came on a regular workday. A call mid-morning from the facility informing me that my mother had fallen earlier in the day getting onto the bus for an outing. I needed to come and take her to the doctor for X-rays. *If she broke her hip, wouldn't she feel the pain?* Apparently, not necessarily. She looked fine to them, but they had spoken with her doctor, and he insisted on X-rays. I canceled the remainder of my meetings for the day and proceeded to her facility.

On a tip from a friend, I had started keeping all medical records, power of attorney, insurance cards, and other necessities in a yellow envelope on top of my refrigerator. After this day, I would also keep a copy in my car, as well as on my phone and on my person because documents on top of your refrigerator serve no purpose when you are not in your kitchen. Keeping them in a cloud drive or, better yet, as a photo will do the trick.

I picked up Mom from the facility. Since she was more comfortable at the facility, we had started visiting there and had not traveled together in a car since her last doctor's appointment several months ago. I had not realized how difficult getting into the car would be. Honestly, I thought

I would ask her to get into the car, and she would get into the car. Maybe it would take her some time to sit in the seat and for me to fasten her seatbelt. In retrospect, how naïve!

I explained how to get in, where to hold while getting in, how you must turn so that your bottom hits the seat, and the function of the seatbelt. I couldn't help thinking that I was perhaps hurting her. *What if she did have a fracture in her hip?* Helping her get into the car and hoping she would not fall was stressful. The seatbelt was confusing. She could not latch herself in the car. We finally maneuvered our way into the car and were on our way.

How can this be? This is the person who helped teach me how to drive a car, how to use a seatbelt. She taught me the most difficult driving skill for a Houstonian: parallel parking. Although I wanted to melt in a puddle of tears, my mom needed to go to the doctor, and I was taking her. We would go to the corner ER, what we liked to call the "Doc in the Box." Between my father, my mother, and myself, we had visited the Doc in the Box many times before.

Once we arrived, the questions started.

I started to talk to the nurse, but she brushed me off. Understandably, she wanted to hear from the patient, not from the patient's adult child. She knew nothing about us. "What is your name?" Blank stare. "I love my children," she said. "Your name. What is your name?" This time a bit more slowly and louder, like she was in a movie talking to someone who spoke a foreign language. No response. "How old are you?" "I love my children," she said. Nothing. An annoyed look shot my way, as if Mom were wasting her time. I explained: "She is not trying to be difficult. She is sick. It's not her fault."

They needed a urine sample and an X-ray. The toilet situation was much like the car:

"I sit on *that*? I do what?!"

"Yes, Mom, you have been doing this for over seventy years. You sit, you leave fluids (don't worry about it—they just come out—and maybe even some solids without effort, if you are lucky and have been eating well), you wipe yourself clean, and then you flush. It's what we humans do. In a toilet. You are a human."

Although I could have been quite upset by the toilet explanation, her reactions were so genuine and surprising, it was impossible to be sad in the moment. She was flabbergasted to hear of this toilet, but eventually sat on it. Nothing happened. We returned to our examining room. It was only later when I reflected on the day that I realized the sadness of the situation.

This reminded me of our last annual appointment. Her doctor has an extremely specific protocol to follow for obtaining a urine sample. The protocol involves opening the container in a certain way, widely spread legs, and two sanitary wipes, which are each used one after the other to clean the exposed area in a circular fashion. He explains it with enthusiasm (and sound effects of how the piss should sound when being released). There is a fist motion that ends the explanation of successful specimen, much like my father used to make for a perfect putt on the golf course. The first time I heard this, I thought the sound effects and fist pumping must have been a one-time thing. Perhaps there is science that the first time you explain a procedure, being animated helps people to remember. Out of my morbid curiosity I asked him to explain the procedure every year. This eventually led to me asking his staff to re-explain it—all I can say is that he teaches his people well. The last time I asked, he gave me two empty urine containers and several wipes so that I could practice at home. He is also my doctor. The first time I attempted the procedure, I peed all over my pants.

During Mom's last appointment, despite her years of training and experience, and the fact that my mother had known the nurse for years, the nurse was unable to obtain a urine specimen from my mother, who did not wish to pull down her pants in front of a stranger. The doctor looked at me and without saying a word, handed me the container and two sanitary wipes.

"I cannot," I said. "There is a line," I insisted. "A very bright, large, permanent marker line," I pleaded.

"You must," he said. "You must try. A clean urine sample is important for her health. She may have a urinary tract infection, and with her Alzheimer's, we would not know. You must. Not a choice, Mary. We will give you some time," he said, and left, pointing to the bathroom.

I felt nauseous. The thought was so disgusting, I did not even feel guilty that my mother's urine would not be tested. We went into the bathroom, and I placed the "helper toilet" over the toilet so that she would not need to bend so far. I explained the procedure (with muted sound effects and fist pumping). After a lot of laughing and explaining, I coaxed her onto the toilet. I opened the receptacle per procedure. I opened the first sanitary wipe and tried to explain the next steps while resisting the urge to vomit.

I saw a bit of her private parts. I will get the sample. I will. If it is for Mom's health, I will do it and pay for a therapist later. I will take prescription drugs to deal with my horror and anxiety. I will keep a journal. I will talk for hours to strangers about my shock and disgust and happily pay them for helping me through this memory. I will do it! For a clean urine sample of my mother to see if she is ill, I will do it. I will put on a persona, act like a doctor treating something she does not know, and I will do it.

To my absolute delight, she said in a very serious and flat voice, the same voice she used when she was mad and referred to me as "Mary Louise" or "Little Missy," "This is not happening." All I could do was thank her. I must have thanked her ten times. *She is in there*—I thought. Feigning sadness, I departed the lavatory, explaining that it just was not going to happen.

I remember specifically the first time my mother did not recognize me. I had heard and read about this moment. I knew it would happen, but it still took me by surprise. At a certain level I did not believe it would happen; Mom and I had been such good friends. There we were on the dreaded fifth floor. My mother was still using a cane—not yet in a wheelchair. When I arrived, she was in the front of the room near the TV watching a movie. I was in the back of the room talking to the nurse about her medications. When I finished talking to the nurse, I took a few steps back to the rear of the room, and I just watched my mother. I guess there was a noise or something because she turned around and looked to the back of the room. We locked eyes. However, the familiarity and recognition I usually received was not there. I was not "The Nice Lady." Instead, she looked through me into the wall behind. I waved and mouthed a shy hello. Nothing. She looked at me with a blank stare, and her eyes left to survey other parts of the room. I was unremarkable.

When I think of this, I can still feel my heart drop into my stomach and feel tears find my eyes. It is a moment etched into my brain. There were so many emotions. As a mother myself, I wondered how a mom could not recognize her child. As a child, I wondered how my mother could not recognize me and the love for her I transmitted through my eyes. After all our trips, conversations, and disagreements, how could she not know I was there? The times we spent together with my children. The lunch and chat we had the day before I returned to work after the birth of my first son. The giggles we exchanged on a regular basis. But her look was vacant, distant. She had no idea who I was. At this moment, I was not her daughter, "The Nice Lady," or even someone vaguely familiar. I was just someone standing in the back of the room. My mom looked through me. I was unremarkable, just a person, just like any other person in the room. Welcome to the disease of Alzheimer's. It sucks.

I wasn't ready for Jane. I desperately needed Mom. I had gotten comfortable with the status quo. The status quo was not perfect, but I had accepted it. It felt like there was no warning of these changes. But there were. You just slowly accept each small step downward and eventually descend to the next level. Some steps are big, and some are so little you don't realize the journey until later, glancing behind your shoulder, you see how far you have gone. You adjust and accept, happy to still be on the trail. You look for the good that remains. And then, before you realize it, you are down to the next level, and on and on and on until there is nowhere else to go, and you are shocked by your descent. You are at the bottom of the ocean. You have somehow seen only the open water, not the green's gradations as the sea floor falls below reefs.

It is hard to lose someone bit by bit, little by little, and not mourn every little loss. In retrospect, you must focus on and be thankful for the present moment. However, focusing on the present is a constant reminder of how much you prefer the past, which makes this extremely difficult!

After my mother's death, I looked at pictures of her in her prime—all that I could find. I was so focused on Jane that I had forgotten how stylish and beautiful Mom was. So, I guess focusing only on the present is not the right answer. The past is also important.

However, as a caregiver, you must also continuously plan for the future. *What will happen next? If she could no longer stay at home, where would she go? What are the health decisions that must be made? What can she afford?*

Being the "meat" of the sandwich generation is a challenge. As a caretaker, you are told to "enjoy your children" and "nurture yourself." These things are also true. You must focus on yourself and your family and try to have your own life. Otherwise, you may feel resentful. Your children also need you. If you are a single parent, then you are trying to navigate a couple's world alone. The list goes on and on, depending upon your specific situation. Just thinking about what to focus on is exhausting. Do the best you can; no one is perfect. Although I constantly tell my boys these things, telling myself is much more difficult.

Be thankful for the present. Remind yourself of the past even if it makes you quite sad. Sometimes you can locate some happiness within the sadness—like a funny memory. Quickly and efficiently plan for the future, as you would make a cold business decision. And make a list of at least three things you could do to take care of yourself: a meditation app, walks, a weekly movie, or just plain silence might help. Look for blogs of others like you. Find a support group. Read. Allow yourself to cry. Try not to turn to alcohol. Such easy things to say, but hard things to do. I wish I had done those things! My fat pants would still fit.

I resisted cleaning out our family home for a long time. I told myself and others that there was no reason to clean out the house. My reasoning was that she may not like her retirement home. She could get kicked out.

She would need a place to go. This made perfect sense initially. After a year of being empty and with my mother happily at her elder care facility, the time had come. Houses need life, or they deteriorate. Maintaining the house was an unnecessary expense. The time had come. My parents lived in their home for forty years. They never cleared it out; they did not know they would be leaving when they left. I knew the process was going to be extremely emotional and difficult.

To me, the family home was the epitome of family—my family. It was my parents' dream home. In a way, the house contained and represented my life. It was the place I lived from the age of six. Decades of holidays, birthdays, parties, laughs, arguments, mischief, and love all occurred within its walls. Perhaps that is the reason I left practically everything intact, as if it were a shrine. The newspaper was just as my father had left it. The radio my mother sometimes listened to at night sat on her bedside table. Groceries purchased were in the pantry. Blue Bell vanilla ice cream cups and vegetables hand-chopped by my mother remained in the freezer—the same freezer where my mother had frozen butter and bologna sandwiches in individual brown lunch bags for me to take to school—because finding time to make lunch had simply become too difficult, and she wanted to focus on her writing more. I recall coming home one day to an assembly line of sandwiches. Apparently, frozen butter on bread works, but frozen mayonnaise does not. After the dreary season of butter sandwiches, I was allowed to purchase my lunch from the school cafeteria.

A confession: I used to visit just to feel the love and warmth of my family home. It was exactly as they had left it (except for the redecoration that occurred prior to Mom's moving to the nursing home). It was a shrine. I sat where my mother used to exercise, when I brought my sons over for a visit. I visited Dr. Grandma Jane's operating table for our plants. I tried to fit in the space under her writing desk as I did when I was a kid, where I would read or do my homework while she would write. I admired her impressive array of office supplies in her office closet. I surveyed the foods in the pantry that she had purchased repeatedly because she didn't remember having purchased them. I laid in the bed where I found my father and wished for a sign from God or someone that he had reached the next realm and was okay. Or maybe even a message that everything would be okay in the future. Afterward I would go home and resume my life. Perhaps I should have found a counselor instead of doing these things. Now that I read what I wrote, it seems a bit warped . . . yet natural. There was no reason to feel so alone. I should have reached out to someone.

The first stage of cleaning out the home occurred when Mom was still living in the home. This stage was focused on safety because anything additional was very upsetting to my mother. I removed old medications and things that could be dangerous, as well as expired foods. I obtained her current medication list from her doctor (which I could do because of the Gift of Documentation) and compared it to the medications in her bathroom. I discovered that my mother had stopped taking her dementia medication, Aricept.[1] My mother also took a thyroid replacement, and I discovered that she was taking an incorrect dosage. Once these matters were corrected, my mother seemed to "bounce back," at least a little bit. "Safety cleaning" was a relatively easy and critical task, which was done while someone took Mom out for an afternoon. Cleaning out a home because no one is living there was much harder.

After the initial stage of safety cleaning, the second stage of cleaning out the house was organizing. When someone has Alzheimer's, items may be placed in surprising and out-of-place locations. Therefore, you must (ideally) carefully look through every nook and cranny. This stage consisted of understanding what items were in the house, what documents could and should be shredded. For myself, the organizational stage was the crying stage. I learned that my parents had kept anything sentimental, such as letters I wrote to them from summer camp at age twelve. I found cute notes written by my father to my mother on mail or random sheets of paper. Tax returns had been kept in paper form and years beyond any necessary date. Hundreds of dollars in change sat in Folgers Coffee cans on the floor of my mother's closet hidden behind clothing. Newspapers had not been thrown away. The grocery shopping must have consisted of the same list each week whether the groceries were necessary or not, creating an abundance of mustard and ziplock bags.

The third stage of cleaning out the house was discussing matters with family members and seeing what people might like to have as a remembrance. We used color-coded sticky notes. Each child had a color, and by a certain date you were required to tag items you wished to keep. As you might imagine, some items had multiple colors. Many items were sentimental. Each time my mother traveled to Mexico she would buy a small decorative frog. Everyone wanted a frog. She created needlepoint butterflies that were made into pillows, another hot item. The dancing figurines that appeared each December. The Christmas train around the tree. The "Children's Bench" from my father's childhood family home. To me it felt like all my happy memories were being ripped apart. It was only when I saw these precious items in the households of my brothers that I realized how wonderful it was that everyone had selected something special to keep. We shared fond memories of our family home, and we each wanted a part of it in ours.

The fourth stage of cleaning out the house is figuring out what you will do with items no one wants. In my case, I hired an estate agent who took a commission of all goods sold. Under her strict protocol, the contract had a date after which you were no longer allowed in the house. Whatever remained was hers to sell. Since the neighborhood did not allow estate sales, she invited people over at a certain date and time for each person. If they happened to see something they wished to purchase, they were free to do so. It was a visit, not an estate sale.

The day before the visitors started arriving, I was asked to walk through the house. They had done a superb job organizing, and even though I thought I had uncovered everything in the house, I had not. There were childhood books of my father for $2 or $5 each. Decorative ceramic eggs that were so carefully selected during family vacations to display in glass cabinets had cheap $2 price tags. Potted plants loved and cared for by my mother were for sale, kitchen utensils, bath towels I used as a child, blankets from my parents' bed. A price tag on my 1980s pink prom dress with an obnoxiously large bow. Entire lives commoditized. I thought the crying stage was over, but it was not.

Many items did not sell. These items were donated to a church whose representatives came and selected what they thought useful.

What remained was a sad reminder that life used to exist in the family home, but that time had passed. Empty rooms. Rooms with a couple of random pieces of furniture. Coffee stains on dark blue carpet for all to see. A portion of a wardrobe. Remnants of things. Things no one wanted—that not even the church wanted for free. In the greatest insult of all, 1-800-GOT-JUNK was called. A payment was made to take these once-loved items. A life now disassembled except for the few items in my mother's new home and sentimental items spread out among children.

I would repeat a simplified and streamlined process of her room years later after her passing. The Salvation Army arrived with a truck. I picked up boxes from the local storage facility. I packed her clothing, towels, and sheets. I shredded anything personal. My siblings and myself selected our keepsakes. When I finished, it was just an empty room that another person would move into. It was a room, I realized, that had already known death and would know it again. Again, I sat where the bed was located and said a prayer. I wished for a sign that she had arrived at her next realm, or a sign of anything that would tell me what happens after death. I thought of the people before her who had lived in this room and their families. Unlike my family home, there would not be the luxury of leaving things in her room to visit what once was. This was not her home, but a room in a nursing facility. By that time, I had grown more accustomed to grief and loss. I would still cry while packing, but the sting was not as harsh. I did not know when cleaning out the house that years would pass until I would clean out her room, and at that time, the world would be amid a pandemic, which does put the importance of a decorative egg, chair, or wall hanging in perspective.

Handling/Supporting Deterioration

Alzheimer's need not destroy all laughs and good times.
Enjoy the time together. Create good memories that you can reflect upon as the disease progresses. Find activities that fit where your loved one is in the journey. Tell your loved one that you love him or her while they still recognize you. Celebrate the activities your loved one can still do. Alzheimer's only gets worse, never better, so don't look back and wish you had done more with your loved one while you still had the opportunity.

Acknowledge and deal with your grief.
There will be a time when your loved one does not recognize you. It is inevitable. This is the disease running its course. You must accept it. Although your loved one does not recognize you, you can still focus on strengthening the emotional connection you have together by holding hands, sitting together, listening to music, or enjoying another activity. This will be difficult, and it is important to take care of yourself. Allow yourself to grieve. My mistake was continuing to move through my day as if things were normal and refusing to acknowledge my grief. Journaling or talking to someone about the experience would have helped me move through it in a healthier way.

Deterioration will not follow the textbook.
Passing from one "stage" of the disease to another will probably not be a clear line; it could be fuzzy or jagged. You have no control over the disease. You have no control over how Alzheimer's disease progresses or how long each stage of the disease will last. You cannot predict the future. Stop trying.

**Activities with your loved one
need not be complicated or elaborate.**
Outings can be simple, uncomplicated affairs – like an outing to the back porch to sit and talk. A brief walk is wonderful while it is still possible.

119

Walking around a neighborhood, park, or backyard is exercise. Listening to music, playing simple card games, and completing simple puzzles are good ideas for activities. Don't put pressure on yourself to have an elaborate outing like to a museum or a movie. These activities may be overstimulating and are harder to execute. Simple outings work, are enjoyable, and are less stressful. The Alzheimer's Association has a list of fifty activities on its website.[2]

Tips for Coping with Grief and Loss

As the disease progresses and your loved one deteriorates, you will continue to feel grief. Below are some helpful tips for coping with grief and loss.

Accept all your feelings.

As the disease continues, you will experience an array of feelings. Love, sadness, guilt, frustration, anger, fear, and relief to name a few. You may even feel resentful at times. Some feelings will be positive, and some feelings will be negative. Accept all these feelings, even if they are conflicting. Feelings of anger and love can exist simultaneously. These are healthy emotions. Don't tell yourself that you "should" feel one way or another.

Expect to feel loss more than once.

When my father passed in his sleep, I felt grief and loss for his death. One day he was here; the next day he was not. It was one—of many—events that caused immeasurable sadness, and I grieved that event. Upon his death I joined a new generation, the sandwich generation, which I knew was life-altering, and I grieved this change in my life. My mother was physically present for over a decade while she slowly lost her abilities. As the disease progressed and her abilities deteriorated, I felt grief and loss repeatedly. Grief that she could no longer cook her favorite meals, drive, talk about current events, write, attend school events, remember my name, know her grandsons, and recognize me, to name a few. Often,

I denied myself feelings of grief because I had already grieved her diagnosis. In grieving the diagnosis of Alzheimer's, hadn't I expunged all feelings of loss associated with the disease? After all, I knew she was living with Alzheimer's, and these further deteriorations were simply part of the disease, a diagnosis I had accepted. Grieving each incremental loss seemed self-indulgent. However, this is not how Alzheimer's works. There is not one loss, but many. In retrospect, I should have accepted and acknowledged those repeated feelings of loss. I now appreciate that they are a normal part of the grieving process for someone living with Alzheimer's.[3]

Everyone grieves differently and at their own pace.

Know that your grieving process may look quite different from someone else's. Grief affects people differently depending upon several factors, such as the length and severity of illness, your own personal experiences, and your relationship with the person living with Alzheimer's. If your grief is so intense that your well-being is at risk, ask for help from your doctor or a professional counselor.

Find an outlet through which to express your feelings.

Talking with a therapist who specializes in grief counseling is an excellent way to express your feelings and receive valuable feedback and suggestions. You may want to interview therapists to select one with whom you are comfortable.

Resist the temptation to settle into feelings of isolation and loneliness.

As a caregiver, it is easy to convince yourself that you have no time for enjoyable activities or hobbies. You also may feel guilty about enjoying yourself. However, it is critical that you force yourself to maintain your friendships and do things that you enjoy. Taking a fun break will put things in perspective and relieve stress. It will also strengthen your support network. If there are activities you enjoy, stay involved. Start with a realistic goal, such as lunch or a movie with a friend, and take it from there.

Join a caregivers' support group.

Share your emotions with other caregivers. Locate an Alzheimer's Association care group on their website. Support groups are not for everyone. If you are uneasy about joining a support group, start by reading the postings of other caregivers on AlzConnected. Knowing that there are other people struggling with the same issues can bring comfort and peace. You might also find some helpful advice.

Accept that some people will not understand your grief.

Many people will believe that since your loved one is living, you should not feel grief. To these people, grief is something that happens when someone dies. They have not experienced loving someone with a progressive cognitive illness and do not know that it is possible to grieve deeply for someone who is still alive.

Treat yourself as you would treat a friend.

Is what you expect from yourself realistic? How would you treat a friend in a similar circumstance? Would you talk to your friend as you talk to yourself? Would you give your friend a hug? If so, give yourself a hug!

Stay healthy.

Staying healthy is one of the best ways you can support your loved one. By staying healthy, you will be happier, stronger, and better able to handle the ups and downs of caring for someone with Alzheimer's. Staying healthy includes taking care of your emotional, mental, and physical well-being. Staying healthy also includes knowing when you need to ask for help and taking the brave step to ask for it.[4]

Token

By Jane P. Moreland

You give me the crystal goblets,
lucent shivery, glistening as they did
for seventy years locked in stagnant air
of the black oak hutch in the front room,
saved treasure of the stocky wonder
who hit the floor with the rooster,
laced bruised, punched leather shoes
formed to the calluses on her feet,
headed up the garage loft to gather eggs
and strangle something for dinner,
who clothed her brood
from a treadle machine in the stale attic,
stomping down narrow steps
to punch botches into the potbellied stove,
who rushed into the wind before rain,
squatting to fill her apron with pecans
as they were hurled to clack in deep grass,
and humming, hulled them into a tin bucket
on warm tile steps of the back stoop.
I would rather have her shoes

Chapter 10

Nourishing Mind, Body, and Spirit: Food, Self-Care, Appearance, Coping Strategies

In their later years, my parents did not go out much, but they did enjoy meals at a neighborhood restaurant called Joyce's. The food is great, and they always saw someone they knew. It is, as we say, a Houston staple.

At the beginning of Mom's deterioration (or at least what I thought was the beginning), the three of us went to Joyce's for a late lunch. My father recognized the couple a few tables over from our intended table but could not remember their names. My mother immediately knew their names and quietly told my father just in time for him to say a polite hello as we passed by their table.

At this time, Mom did not require any assistance with her bathing or wardrobe. She dressed herself in her usual, somewhat-formal attire. Her makeup was flawless. She could hold a conversation and was generally in a very positive mood. She had no difficulty recognizing me or my siblings. An outsider would have had no indication of her illness. She looked at the menu and announced that she would order her favorite dish at Joyce's, the fried shrimp. A minute later, my father asked, "What are you having again, dear?"

She could not remember and looked at the menu. "Fried shrimp," she said. She was determined to remember her order when the waiter arrived. The waiter arrived a few minutes later and asked for her order. She had no idea and started laughing. "What am I having, dear?" We all started laughing. "Fried shrimp," my father informed the waiter.

After Dad passed away, but Mom still lived at home, we would go out to eat on special occasions, such as when relatives came to visit. My mother would study the menu and decide what she wanted to order. When the waiter came around, she always seemed to order whatever the person next to her ordered. "You know, I changed my mind. I will also have the _____. That sounds so good!" Preparing meals at home was a group effort. Mom would show others how to cook her favorite dishes, while her helpers kept track of measurements and cooking times. There is something so comforting about eating your favorite dish. I know that she greatly enjoyed these mouthfuls of memories.

When she lived in assisted care before moving to the memory care floor, we would eat together downstairs at the restaurant, where cheerful waiters would help us. She would stare at the menu with a blank look.

"Mom, look, they have shrimp. Would you like that?"

"Oh, yes, definitely. Thank you!"

As she deteriorated, the staff at the assisted home facility would say, "Jane, would you like the Special today?"

"Oh, yes, please."

Later they would not ask and just serve. Once when I sat at the table, they informed me that Jane always liked to have the Special of the Day. It was her "standing order." Coincidentally, everyone at the table had the same standing order.

Once she moved to the memory care floor, there was no longer the façade of a choice. A cart of food was rolled in, and staff wearing clear gloves made identical plates for all using ice cream scoops and large spoons, unless someone was on a restricted menu. They no longer ate in the restaurant, but in a room on their floor. Their lives were condensed to the dreaded fifth floor, classes sometimes on the fourth floor, occasional trips to the beauty parlor within the building, and trips to the fenced-in garden. There were no outings in the van to a museum or a restaurant. A real *Groundhog Day* existence.

My mother took pride in her appearance. Her nails were almost always painted in a nude shade, which she insisted on doing herself, as nail salons must surely have germs. Her hair never turned gray and was always the most beautiful shade of a complex brown with slight red or blonde undertones depending upon her mood. Her lips were a tasteful, classic red. She always looked put-together and glamorous.

It was not until my mid-forties that I appreciated makeup. The art of makeup alluded me in my youth, and I did not understand why my teenage face (and skin) needed it. In response, my mother summoned a "Color Me Beautiful" representative who showed up one day—to my surprise—to assist her daughter to look a bit more "ladylike." The representative "did my colors" and tried to teach me the art of putting on makeup. I was furious. I refused to wear the makeup, which sat unused in a drawer for months. It was the teenage equivalent of banishing caregivers to the upstairs or sticking my tongue out when asked if I took my medicine.

Mom wore the same shade of Revlon lipstick for decades. When she was at the nursing home, I recall being in Walgreens replenishing her lipstick, and the Color Me Beautiful day bounced into my brain. I wanted so badly to apologize for my actions and childish behavior, but Jane would not have understood. I purchased the lipstick and returned to the facility. Jane was delighted with the new red lipstick. Although she did not exactly know what to do with it, her eyes lit up when I twisted the tube and red popped up.

Mom visited the same hair salon for years. She always had a definite opinion about her hair. She regularly chatted with her stylist about life, children, and anything else that was relevant. Once she began deteriorating, she just went along. Her stylist knew what she liked and just did it. Mom was used to the routine.

Once the Alzheimer's progressed a bit more, someone needed to sit in the salon with her. I remember going one day and the stylist asking me what was wrong. Mom had changed. They no longer chatted about their children, the weather, or plants. Mom did not talk about her grandchildren. The steps in the hair beautification process were confusing. I explained the situation. Like so many people, she had experienced a relative with a form of dementia. The stylist was gracious, and we continued to return until Mom moved to assisted living. Mom may not have understood fully what was going on around her, but her hair looked fabulous!

In the nursing home, the beauty parlor was abuzz with activity. My mother and many of her friends had five alarm red or bright pink painted nails: high-maintenance nail colors my mother would never have chosen. There were hardly any gray heads, despite their ages. However, rather than a soft brown with red undertones, my mother's hair was black. In fact, everyone's hair color was slightly off: a red was a harsh pop-star red. Dark blonde was a single tone of mahogany brown. Brown was jet black. No one noticed. "What pretty red nails!" "Jane, I see you went to the beauty parlor." If there were nothing to chat about, hair color, nail color, and what the weather looked like outside the shut and locked window were tried and true topics. Jane was happy to receive the compliments. Her nicely combed hair and trimmed cuticles boosted her attitude. She did not realize it was all a bit off, or that the manicure was probably more about health than about color.

Her doctor once told me that often Alzheimer's can be more difficult for the loved ones than for the person living with Alzheimer's. In my mother's case, at a certain point I think that was true, because she seemed oblivious to her *Groundhog Day* existence. She did not remember she was a writer. She did not remember traveling. While she still laughed and found joy in happenings around her, our conversations were simple affairs. She might answer a question with a one-word response or not at all. As the observer, you remember the complexities and layers of your loved one, their opinions, their hobbies, and their likes and dislikes. It's hard to see a physical person who no longer connects with the mind of the person you love. The hands are the same, but they can no longer cook or write. However, you can still hold those same hands.

Grief for the loss of our parents is normal. The generations pass. The younger ones are left standing. We learn from our parents—assuming they have been good parents. If they have not, we learn from our friends and role models. Occasionally I wonder, *If I died, would I be with my parents? Would I live a life of my youth?* I miss them immensely.

I have also made some very poor and emotionally painful decisions in recent years. I so wish either of my parents had been mentally capable during those dark times. Thinking about those times makes me afraid. In fact, any bad decision I have made in recent history makes me afraid. Although I believe I have good judgment in general, without the guidance of loved ones, *How will I continue to make good decisions and not fall off the path with a bad one when the going gets tough?* My father always said that when the going gets tough, the tough get going. I just want to make sure I am going in the correct direction!

If I could relive parts of my life, I would pay more attention to my friendships. I used to meet so many interesting people. There were opportunities for so many friends. However, I was always busy or occupied. Work took priority over my personal life. Sometimes I was just overwhelmed being a single mom and caregiver, and I preferred to stay home rather than go to a party or out to a dinner. Over time, there were no more party or dinner invitations.

Maintaining those friendships would have helped me to have someone to talk to, to laugh with, to express my feelings. I would have had a sounding board of people with similar interests. I would have been less insulated. It gets harder and harder to make friends after you have lived in a tunnel. Being isolated in terms of taking care of your children and taking care of your mother is not healthy. The fact that you want a life does not mean you love your children or parent less.

You must take care of yourself. I see now that it is okay to take care of yourself. I have read so many books reminding me of the rules on an airplane—the oxygen mask is for you and then your child. However, I also appreciate that when you have young children, taking care of yourself can seem self-indulgent and expensive. I used to take my kids to the YMCA for "parent's night out." For a reasonable fee, I had four hours to myself. That was wonderful. I could have dinner with a friend or go see a movie. To be honest, most of the time I just came home. I am not sure that was the best choice. You must have your own life. It is your sanity, and the airplane analogy is true. The return of "normal life" after COVID presents a great opportunity to change.

Nourishing Mind, Body, and Spirit

Take time for yourself and keep healthy.
You may have so many responsibilities (particularly if you are in the sandwich generation) that taking time for yourself or doing something that you enjoy may feel self-indulgent, but it is not. The best thing you can do for yourself and your loved one is stay positive, energetic, and strong, and you can only do this if you are taking care of yourself! If you have private caregivers or your loved one lives in a facility, you may feel like you do not deserve a break. After all, you are not with your loved one all day, and they may not live with you. But this is wrong; you also deserve a break! There is an emotional toll with Alzheimer's, and you are no doubt in charge of a long list of responsibilities. We all intend to take time for ourselves, but life so often intervenes. There is always something that must be done! Set a schedule for "me time" and mark it on your calendar. Otherwise, you may never take it. The fact that you want a life does not mean you love your parents or children any less.

Don't second-guess or "revisit" past decisions regarding your loved one's care.
Your loved one's needs will change as the disease progresses. What works well at one stage of the disease may not work at all at later stages. You have no control over how Alzheimer's progresses or how long each stage of the disease will last. This lack of control will make you feel powerless and hopeless. But you cannot predict the future. Often it took me a while to realize that a change in care was necessary due to Mom's deterioration, and I was very critical of myself for not having been more observant.

If you have genuinely tried your best, don't second-guess the decisions you have made about your loved one's care. You also cannot reverse the disease's progression even though you desperately want to do so. All you can do is your best; if you have done your best, you can feel proud.

Get your network in place.

Create a network—a list of people you could call on if you need assistance picking a child up from school, picking up medications, etc. Once you have your ideal list, have a quick conversation with the people on your list. Socialize the idea. Tell them about your idea of creating a network and that you would like for them to be on the list. If you are able, offer to be on their list if they also need assistance. See how they react. You might be surprised by how many people are willing to help you in a pinch. If someone is not amenable to helping you, knowing that before an emergency arises will allow you to exclude them from your list. If they are unable or would prefer not to be on your list, knowing this before a crisis will save time and reduce stress. Having a brief conversation will also make it more difficult for your network to say no when you need them.

It is much easier to pull out your list rather than thinking of whom to call in a crisis. Maybe there is another parent or someone else caring for a loved one, and you could each be on each other's lists. If you do not have a list, then join an Alzheimer's Association support group and ask people how they balance the demands on their time. You might get some good tips, and at a minimum, you will relate to what you hear. If you are a single parent, try to find another single parent and babysit each other's kids. Doing so might enable you to have "me time" without having to pay a babysitter.

Accept that you must be flexible.

You will need to adapt to the disease. A meal in a noisy restaurant may become too stimulating, but a simple meal in a quiet place might still be enjoyable.

Don't neglect your friendships.
It gets harder and harder to make friends after you live in a tunnel. Dig yourself out! Return of "normal life" after COVID creates a great opportunity to become more social.

BOTANICA

By Jane P. Moreland

was the language my mother shared
before I knew words: soft petals
on my cheek, scent of shallots
in wet earth, tastes of fig and lemon.

She coiled my hand around dahlia stems
to make a nosegay, tucked curly ferns
behind my ear, kissed my nose with asters,
sprinkled seeds from ripe pods into my hands.

In her arms I danced
among the willow's limber limbs,
plucked bright gourds from a trellis, hid
from the world in deep cedar shade.

When I was older, we dug side by side,
arms in dirt to elbows among the tangled roots
that steadied stalk and bloom, sliding sisal mats
along the strict borders of bricked beds
as she taught me the rest of it.

Chapter 11

Staying True to Your Loved One: End-of-Life Care

When COVID hit, I was terrified. There had always been a low buzz of worry in the back of my mind, but now there was COVID worry. Since I could not visit my mother, I coped by buying large quantities of "female underwear"—Alzheimer's toilet paper, much of which remains in a storage closet, the final evidence of my caretaking days. COVID has warped time. I spent so much time worrying about Jane, but one day turned into the next and then the next.

I am used to being in control. In fact, a common complaint I have heard throughout my life is my apparent insistence on being in control of every situation. Control brings me security and warmth. Control brings managed expectations. Control brings predictability. With Alzheimer's there is no control. Only self-doubt and guilt, even if you should not feel those emotions.

I kept remining myself during the pandemic that I should not feel guilty about not visiting Mom. For once in my life, I should not feel guilty about not seeing her more often—it literally was not legally allowed. I kept telling myself that this fact should provide me with a sense of freedom, but it did not. I worried constantly. I wanted to know whether she was alright. Despite the legal restrictions, I continued feeling guilty. Video chats are difficult with someone who is confused and doesn't know you. Even though I logically knew she did not, I wondered if she missed The Nice Lady. *Did she think The Nice Lady had abandoned her?* My paranoia made me wonder if people were still as nice to residents when there were no visitors around.

Mom was negative after the first round of COVID tests. This was such a relief. Of course, she was negative! My mother for decades ate an apple a day, put flax on her cereal, lifted weights, rode her stationary bike, exercised her mind, and did sit-ups. *We have avoided COVID*, I confidently thought. *They will follow protocols, and all will be just fine.*

On an ordinary day in May 2020, I received a call from a Pal at the nursing home who was "contact tracing," asking in a light, happy voice for my permission to test my mother for COVID. It took several minutes for the weight of that request to sink in—obviously, my mother had been in close contact with an infected person. Someone where she lived had COVID. COVID was back in the building. Mom needed testing. She could have been infected. Still, I was confident that she would be negative—*how "close" could she have gotten to another resident?* By that time, she was in a wheelchair. What I had not thought of was the Pals and caretakers themselves—who live their lives as we all do, shop at the grocery store, and are our frontline workers. These Pals brushed her teeth, bathed her, and helped her eat. These events do not occur six feet away. It was only a matter of time until contagious COVID again reared its ugly head.

She was positive. At first, she was not exhibiting symptoms. I learned that many residents with COVID had no symptoms. She then took a turn for the worse. The phone call came. They were putting her in an ambulance to go to the hospital. "Do you have a preference of hospitals?" they asked. Having visited a few hospitals with my mother in the past, I did.

Despite my requests, I was not allowed to go with her. I would need to call the emergency room after her arrival to make sure they had all her paperwork and talk to a nurse. They advised to wait a few hours so that the hospital could put her in the records; the nursing home would send a folder with her documentation. I waited a couple of difficult hours and then called the emergency room nurse. To feel useful, and because I did not trust that all paperwork had arrived, I arranged to bring the paperwork to the hospital. The hospital was very busy. In the background, I could hear sounds of beeps and a woman's voice on the intercom: "Code Blue."

Mom was at the hospital without a friend or advocate. She was alone with annoying beeping sounds. *Was she afraid? Was she on oxygen?* At that time, COVID seemed like a death sentence. I had seen my mother for the last time. I would never see my mother alive again. She would die alone like so many people who died alone in hospitals with COVID. If we were lucky, we would get to see her through a phone screen. I would never hold her elegant hand again.

Despite her doctor's advice and her advanced Alzheimer's, I was convinced that before death she would have a moment of lucidity. She would know me. I would thank her. We would tell each other "I love you." Selfishly and illogically, I mourned the possibility of a life without telling her goodbye in her moment of clarity. I petitioned to be able to see her, but I was denied. I rationalized that being denied was a very positive sign. A victory. *Why would I need to obtain emergency approval to visit her?* She is improving, and the doctors know she will recover. Therefore, they did not approve my petition. This is an exceptionally good sign. The mind sees what we want to be true.

After what seemed like an eternity full of ICU beds, tests, talks of stomach plugs, PICC lines and antibiotics, she became medically stable, but remained COVID positive. The hospital needed to move her out of the COVID ward. Mom needed to leave the hospital. Her facility refused to allow her to return until she was COVID negative for fourteen days. She was a temporarily homeless, eighty-one-year-old woman living with Alzheimer's who was now only transportable by ambulance. She needed greater medical care than her nursing facility provided. I looked for a skilled nursing facility, a facility somewhere in between a hospital and a nursing home. Finding a place that would take COVID patients took many phone calls. There were no tours or in-person meetings allowed. You placed your mother in the care of strangers with a leap of faith. Sure, an internet review told you some things, but there is nothing like seeing a place, eating a meal, and asking questions. I found a facility about thirty miles away with a COVID ward. They had a bed and would take her. My phone calls asking how she was were not returned. Most calls were never answered. Rings to nowhere. Promises of video conferences were broken. All I could do was sit and worry in my house and continue calling to learn something about the status of my mother. I dropped off clothing for Mom and chatted with the exhausted nurses working on the COVID ward. They wanted to return phone calls. They were understaffed. The frontline workers were overwhelmed. Several people had quit. Mom was fine. They would send me a picture. I needed to drop off her suitcase and leave. In this instance, no news was good news. If she were crashing, I would be called. I was able to have a brief conversation with them about her likes, dislikes, and health, which would have to suffice.

From May through November 2020, she was in and out of hospitals, contracted COVID twice, had repeated urinary tract infections, was septic twice, and was passed between her nursing home, hospitals, and skilled facility multiple times.

As a caregiver of a person living with Alzheimer's, you learn that your loved one needs an advocate in the hospital. The advocate can talk to the doctors, explain your loved one's condition, and generally make things more comfortable for your loved one. The advocate can make sure food is cut into smaller pieces and that your loved one eats. The advocate might be able to tell when your loved one is in pain and communicate that fact to the medical staff who do not know your loved one well. Some hospitals might provide a helper free of charge overnight, so that you can rest.

Not being able to advocate for her in all these places was agony. "Your mother seems a little confused," the nurse would inform me over the phone amid the beeps of medical equipment and announcements over the intercom in the hospital. They were concerned about her not eating—several "swallow tests" were administered, although I think she may have just needed someone to prompt her to eat, help her with the spoon or fork, or feed her in small bite sizes. There were talks of a permanent feeding plug or tube, two things she would not have wanted. "She could not tell me her name," said a nurse. "I asked her if she was in pain, and she did not say she was in pain," said another. One assumes all medical professionals have experience with dementia and Alzheimer's, but they do not. Of course, they may not have even known of her Alzheimer's, as in the past, I needed to explain the situation, and I am sure they were all quite overwhelmed with COVID.

When I finally was able to see her, I was in full PPE on the intensive care floor of the hospital and held her hand through a thick purple glove. I had not seen her in person for almost six months, the longest time in my life that I had not seen my mother. There she was almost in a fetal position. She was laying on her side in a hospital gown with a pillow between her knees. She looked terrible and was sleeping most of the time. She had not been sent with any clothing or toiletries. The outfit she had worn in the ambulance was on a shelf in the corner. A hospital-issued toiletry bag was next to her clothes. Her room was small with a loud air conditioning unit in the back of the room. Signs covered the doorway informing all staff and visitors to don full PPE. Eventually she looked at me with a blank stare. She was alive by the grace of modern medicine and antibiotics. I held her hand and stroked her cheek through my glove. I think she liked the sound of my voice.

She eventually returned to her home on a liquid diet and without a feeding plug or tube. My sons and I visited her behind plexiglass the day after she returned to her nursing home. The Pal put a walkie talkie in her hand to communicate with me. Bewildered, she stared at the walkie talkie. Annoyed, she listened to and winced at the squeals of the speaker. I got someone to turn it off. Relative to the intensive care unit, she looked wonderful. I took a video while my sons and I smiled behind our masks and waved. At the time I thought she smiled back, but now that I look at the video, I think it perhaps was just a reflex. It was clear she had deteriorated during the past six months. Looking at the video several months later I notice that her clothes are too large due to the amount of weight she lost, her skin looks pale, and she is leaning against the side of the wheelchair rather than holding herself up straight. Her expression in the video is distant.

I could not see the back of her head, but they told me that her hair was matted from constantly being in the bed at the skilled care facility. Apparently, she may have never left her bed. The Pal suggested cutting off the matted hair. Knowing how she felt about her appearance and particularly her hair, I offered to come back without my children and comb out her tangles. I was happy to sign any liability waiver regarding COVID that they required. I reminded them of my lawyer status and that I fully understood the legal documentation. I would wear gloves and a mask, multiple masks if they preferred. I could put on full PPE. I could comb her hair outside in the garden. Denied. We settled on my returning with a bottle of full-strength detangler. Mom was oblivious to the entire exchange, which occurred immediately in front of her.

I was able to visit with her two additional times behind plexiglass. Each time I declined the thoughtful walkie talkie and speaker. For the last visit I brought a David Sedaris book, one of her favorite authors, and started to read, but then became teary eyed and stopped. *Why did I think the book was a good idea?* A Pal noticed that I was upset and sat behind her and told her what to say: "Say, I love you."

"I love you," she repeated in a flat voice like a parrot.

While I appreciated the Pal's effort, it just made me feel worse. There obviously was something going on in her brain to repeat the message. She was not entirely gone, yet she still did not recognize me or understand the words. I don't think she noticed the plexiglass structure between us. You always think you have hit bottom with Alzheimer's, until you take yet another step downhill. She stared at me blankly while I told her I loved her, smiled, and blew kisses.

When her doctor mentioned the idea of hospice, I was not ready. In fact, I was offended! But he was correct. I had always thought hospice was a death sentence, but I was informed that many people on the memory care floor had been on hospice for quite a while and still left their rooms, ate with the group, and led a similar life to their pre-hospice lives. It just meant that the next time she became ill, the focus would be on comfort, not on pumping strong antibiotics through an IV to sustain her life.

As a single parent with two teenage boys, I was worried about myself once Mom was placed on hospice. My children are not my therapists. I desperately needed someone to talk to about my mother, but I was the only adult in the house. I had tried video therapy before, but it was hard to connect over the computer screen. I googled and located a highly rated site and purchased weekly visits for several months. Although I was not hopeful, I needed the voice and reason of an adult. I finally reached out for the help I needed with the attitude required to receive it.

There is a doctor behind "hospice." I met with him after I signed the hospice contract. We discussed Mom's wishes. We discussed in detail medical treatment that would be administered and treatment that would not. We reviewed her medications together and decided what would continue and what would not. We reviewed legal documentation together. We talked about chain of command and who was legally empowered to make decisions. We agreed upon a communication plan. He introduced me to the case manager who would oversee Mom's care. I recall feeling sad and incredibly lonely. He told me he was available twenty-four seven and insisted I put his number and the case manager's number in my phone during the meeting while he watched even though I said I would do it later. Although I knew deep in my heart that putting my mother on hospice would be the beginning of the end, I allowed myself the luxury of thinking this was not so. She would bounce back; I was sure of it. I had visions of noodle classes and duck paintings. She would enjoy life. Laugh. Hug me. Maybe even know who I was.

Planning for End of Life

Consider palliative or hospice care earlier than you think necessary.

Talk to your loved one's doctor about these services. A common misconception is that hospice care is only available when death is very near. However, this is not necessarily the case. Palliative care might also be a helpful option before your loved one qualifies for hospice care. Both palliative and hospice service offer help and guidance for you, the caregiver, in addition to your loved one. General information about these services appears below:

- **What is palliative care?** Palliative care is a type of medical care for people with a serious illness, including Alzheimer's dementia. It can be started at any phase of the disease. Palliative care aims to improve quality of life not only for the person living with Alzheimer's, but also for the caregiver. In addition to helping your loved one, having an available resource familiar with Alzheimer's dementia can better equip you to deal with difficult situations. Palliative care providers work with your existing health care provider; you are not required to give up your existing provider when you begin palliative care. Before engaging a palliative care provider, however, you should check with your insurance provider (whether your provider is Medicare or a private health insurer) to confirm what costs will be covered.[1] Below is a list of services that palliative care may include:
    - Management of Alzheimer's symptoms, such as depression, restlessness, anxiety, and trouble sleeping
    - Assistance for the family in developing an overall care plan for your loved one
    - Coordination of health care with other providers
    - Education for the family about advance directives, strategies, and techniques for avoiding triggers of Alzheimer's symptoms, and making decisions about living arrangements
    - Assistance completing insurance forms
    - Care related to emotional and spiritual needs, if desired[2]

- **What is hospice care?** Unlike palliative care, which can be implemented at any phase of a serious illness, hospice care is implemented in the final stages of illness before death. During hospice care, medical doctors discontinue curative treatment for disease and instead focus solely on managing pain and symptoms of the disease.[3] For example, in my mother's case, she stopped receiving medications to treat her dementia, but continued to receive anti-anxiety medication. The goal of hospice care is to minimize pain and discomfort and maximize life in the final stages of illness.[4] Hospice care also includes palliative care (described above) as well as additional benefits.

- Management of symptoms, such as medications for pain control and anxiety
- Nursing and medical staff
- Assistance for families in understanding the dying process and coping with grief; for example, after my mother's death, I received several phone calls from our provider checking to see how I was doing, in addition to offers of counseling and literature about the grieving process
- Medical equipment—my mother's provider brought in a new hospital bed and a high-back wheelchair
- Assistance with certain daily activities, such as bathing[5]

- **Is hospice care covered by Medicare?** It is important to ask if the hospice provider is Medicare Approved. Hospice providers that are Medicare Approved will be covered by Medicare.[6]

- **What are the requirements for a person diagnosed with Alzheimer's to receive hospice covered by Medicare?**
  - Eligibility. The individual is eligible for Medicare Part A.
  - Certification. For Medicare to cover hospice care, the individual's medical doctor and the hospice doctor must certify that the individual is terminally ill. In this context, "terminally ill" means a life expectancy of six months or less, assuming the illness continues along its normal course. In the context of dementia, including Alzheimer's dementia, there are guidelines published by the National Hospice and Palliative Care Organization to assist in determining

whether the individual has a prognosis of six months or less.[7] However, keep in mind that these are only guidelines. In any event, the determination of life expectancy is made by a medical professional, not you.

- ◆ Waiver and election. The individual (or the individual's representative, for example, under a health care power of attorney) waives the right for Medicare to pay for medications and care relating to treatment of the underlying condition and elects to receive hospice care. Notwithstanding this waiver, Medicare will continue to pay for covered benefits that are not related to treatment of the underlying disease.[8]

- **Is there a limit on the amount of time that a person living with Alzheimer's can receive hospice services under Medicare?** An individual with Alzheimer's dementia may elect to receive hospice care for two ninety-day benefit periods. After these two ninety-day periods, the individual may continue to receive hospice services for an unlimited number of sixty-day benefit periods. For each period, the hospice physician must provide a recertification that the individual continues to be qualified for hospice services.[9]

Questions to ask when interviewing a hospice provider:
- Are you Medicare-certified?
- What licenses and accreditations do you have?
- Ask for references.
- What experience do you have caring for someone living with Alzheimer's or other dementias?
- What current medications or treatments would be stopped, if any?
- Are there any out-of-pocket expenses I should expect?
- Are there any services, equipment, or medication that you do not provide?
- How often will your staff visit my loved one? Is there a schedule for visits?

- How long will a typical visit last?
- Will the frequency of visits change as my loved one's health declines?
- Who will visit my loved one? Will someone be assigned to my loved one, or is there a rotation of staff?
- How will you keep me informed of my loved one's health, and how often?
- If your loved one is living in a nursing facility, ask if the provider assists other residents at the facility. Do they assist people on the memory care floor? Assisting other residents in the facility might mean their representatives are more readily available should you need help. Cross-check the response with the facility's management, who should also have this information. Although no one will provide you with detailed information due to privacy concerns, the hospice company and the nursing facility should be able to provide you with general information.
- What will happen if there is an emergency?
- What if an emergency occurs after regular business hours?
- How will I reach you twenty-four seven?
- What bereavement services do you offer?
- Do you offer respite care and under what circumstances?
- What other services do you provide? At what cost?
- What makes you different from other hospice providers? Why should I choose you for such an important and personal role?

Upon engaging hospice care, I suggest that you ask for the number(s) of your twenty-four-hour, seven-days-a-week contact and immediately put the contact information into your phone. You will have questions and concerns; make it easy for yourself and ask the questions you need to ask. Experiencing the death of a loved one is traumatic. The last thing you want to be doing at such an emotionally charged time is fumbling for a telephone number.

IN PINE SHADE

By Jane P. Moreland

My mother's dying room today is darker
with cedars merged outside her windows,
ivy up another inch on screens.
In this dim light, we could be in shade
of pines at her back fence, where for years
we cooled with pitchers of ice water
after weeding flower beds in summer sun.

I have brought a bouquet from that garden
of neglect and straggles, hungry for her hands,
garden of warm days and cool evenings
that have allowed summer and fall to overlap
with coral vine and ginger gone rank, verbena
spilling over brick borders, honeysuckle
blanketing new shoots of tulips and hyacinths,
buds of red quince set tight along bare stems.

She touches the bouquet to her cheek,
begins softly to name each flower: blue iris
we planted last birthday, wisteria
dug one spring from a roadside ditch,
crepe myrtle that rained florets over okra
we planted the summer I was eight, tea roses
my father brought when I was born, seeing
with joy as we move along the taproot
of memory as if to a telescope's tapering end,
to the ocular, and then through it to her dream
of me in a field of indigo just before
the gleam in time when we began.

Saying Goodbye

The first few days of hospice have been wonderful. Mom looks peaceful and happy. She is clean, smells fresh, and is covered head to toe in moisturizer. Her teeth are brushed. Her hair has long gray roots but is neat and combed without tangles. She bid farewell to a liquid diet and ate on her own. She ate entire meals. Many of the Pals stopped by to visit. Mom thanked the Pals for adjusting her pillow and helping her eat. She enjoyed desserts. She was alert (relatively) and even watched some Hallmark channel. Hospice ordered her the most comfortable hospital bed and a high-back wheelchair that they said was needed for when she returned to the social schedule. There is an expectation that she will return to her classes and activities. The case manager is attentive and loving. She brought little tubes for Mom to grip so that she would be more comfortable. I qualify as an "essential visitor" and am allowed to visit her in her room. Her nursing home gave me the code to the door to her floor and lets me come and go as I please, day or night. Today, I held Mom's hand without a glove. Her bed has clean sheets and a sunflower blanket. We made eye contact. Life is good!

Monday, November 23, 2020

I got some bad news about my mother yesterday. She needed oxygen and had a fever. However, today she perked up, and it was all good news. She ate and was in good spirits. I know she will bounce back. She always bounces back. *What's a little oxygen between friends?*

Thursday, November 26, 2020

My mother has been on hospice for several days. Her voice is now faint. She continues to be on oxygen. Today she let me hold her hand. She mumbled words with intention, holding eye contact, but they made no sense. I tried to understand what she was saying, but it was gibberish. It seemed like she was trying very hard to tell me something. I was frustrated not being able to decode the message.

She wanted something to drink. I lifted the straw of the cup of apple juice to her mouth—she sucked while looking at me, but her sucking was not strong enough to bring the juice to her mouth. Her expression looked like she thought she had drunk fluids, so with a kind smile I put the cup down, knowing the liquid did not make it to her lips.

Occasionally she said yes, no, thank you. She looks tired and weak. She is pale. Despite a new high-back wheelchair waiting to take her to her classes, she has remained in the bed since she returned from a skilled facility about a week ago. I told her how much I love her. I cleaned out part of her closet to be useful. She will appreciate a neat closet when she feels better! She has always bounced back—she survived COVID twice!

I miss her. I miss her laugh and smile, her sense of humor and her warmth. When I visited with her today, I felt like there was something she wanted to say, but that she just couldn't say it. We stared into each other's eyes calmly without speaking for at least fifteen minutes. I wondered if I looked familiar. Sitting, looking at each other, and holding hands was peaceful.

I have realized that my mother will not be here a year from now. She has been here all my fifty-two years. My children are in high school. They will leave for college in a few short years. I always thought my mom would be here a while longer. I thought she would come with me to their high school graduation. I thought she would know where they went to college. I thought we would take trips together—me, Mom, and my boys. She might even meet a great-grandchild one day. I thought we would see our plants grow into great bushes and trees after following Dr. Grandma

Jane's advice. Perhaps we would learn enough during our visits that we would no longer need regular appointments with Dr. Grandma Jane.

But I realize that these dreams died long ago. Mom is weak. She has advanced Alzheimer's. She should be allowed to pass to her next realm. My desperately wanting to return to the past will not make it so. Staring into her eyes will not make her recognize me or heal her brain.

On the one hand, I guess it will be an opportunity to do things I might like to do in my newly acquired free time while I am still relatively young; on the other hand, I am worried I will be lost. Taking care of others is what I do best. Taking care of my mother was part of my purpose. Although I work full-time, taking care of my children is my number one job. I never thought of a time after that; it all seemed so far away. But things are changing before me, and I can't slow anything down. *Who will I become?* And then the guilt of thinking beyond Mom sets in. There has been no trouble crying today, or yesterday. *Why am I crying so much now?* I have known this is coming. I haven't been able to carry on a conversation with her for years. My children have not been able to converse with her. Yet, I am devastated. My mother. My mom. It makes me think of my grandmother and how I didn't really appreciate the effect of her death on my own mom—and I want to tell her all about it and really listen to her tell me how she felt and dealt with it.

I am in menopause, and I want to ask her about it. I will in a few years be an empty nester, and I want to know how she handled that transition. Maybe I should have thought to ask these things before she became so confused, but the inevitable seemed so far away. I wished we had talked about substance rather than the silly subjects that entertained us. However, at the same time, we enjoyed our mindless banter. Despite watching her slow decline for almost a decade, I feel completely unprepared and alone.

I need help. I have realized that I no longer have a support system. So much grief. So many tears are flowing. In the last few years, I haven't kept up with friends or relatives. In retrospect, I wish I had forced myself to do more social activities, to maintain friendships and meet new people. Writing in a journal and talking to a counselor help, but I need more of a life!

Saturday, November 28, 2020

Yesterday when I saw my mother, I thought I was literally seeing someone die before my eyes. When I arrived, she was alone in her room. Her body jerked slightly every few seconds. Her eyes stared at me and then rolled into the back of her head like a kid who can't stay awake in class at school. I looked for the floor nurse. I tried to contact the hospice nurse—no answer. I contacted the hospice doctor and informed him how different Mom was from the day before—his response: "Yes. This is sad." I didn't understand. I asked him to send the nurse. *What is happening?* This isn't the death I know from the movies. In the movies, people drift off to a peaceful sleep. There is no jerking or rolling eyes.

Some think she will bounce back. "It's late in the day. In the morning, she will be better. Things can change hour to hour with Mom." There is truth in those statements. I normally avoid the fifth floor after 3:00 p.m. Things change on the memory care floor late in the day, but then they are back to normal in the morning.

This is different. I can feel it. I see it. In some ways I feel guilty saying it, but I want it—because I watched her twitch, her eyes rolling into the back of her head, her hands clammy, her head hot, the fright in her face when they rolled her over to give her Tylenol and change her underwear, her look of shock that someone is touching her intimate parts. As much as I love her, she would not want this. When I think these thoughts, I feel like a horrible human being. A real mommy killer.

Her doctor had told us that at this stage of the disease Jane would have no idea what is going on and would not recognize our presence. Maybe I am torturing myself by planning to spend as much time as possible with her. Well, I know I am in denial, but I refuse to believe it—surely there is something about my energy, smell, or touch that seems familiar on some level. Plus, even if she has no idea who I am, it is nice to have someone hold your hand, stroke your face, and just be there with you. I do not like the thought of her alone. My father would have wanted someone there. Someone needs to advocate for her.

I'm a train wreck. I have so many different emotions swirling in my head. So many memories of my mother that I haven't thought of in decades bubbling to the surface like a carbonated beverage.

My mother took full advantage of the classes where she lives. Yesterday was surreal. I joke with friends frequently about the swimming noodles which commonly pop up in classes. So many things creative people can do with swimming noodles. "She will be back to noodle chair exercise in no time." She was an A+ noodle exerciser. While I was waiting for the hospice nurse, I left to go to the restroom. There they were: all the residents playing some noodle game and listening to music. Red noodles. Yellow noodles. Green noodles. So many. It made me think—*all the time Mom was noodling, was there someone in a room down the hall dying?*

Probably so, I guess. What a realization.

Part of the pain of Alzheimer's is that you see other people deteriorate as well. Mom started with a group of ladies—when she was on the assisted living floor, they would eat together. When Mom moved to the memory care floor, she moved with the group. We, along with the facility, liked the fact that she would move with her pack. Now, I look around, and almost none have survived. One friend constantly flirted with any male employee ("Hey, good looking, what's cooking?"). Another looked like the school librarian and blushed when you said she looked pretty. A third was very possessive of Mom—I watched them all deteriorate. Now it seems they are gone. *Was it COVID? When? How?* I will never know. *Did they move? Are they alive?*

Alzheimer's is such a cruel, relentless disease. I can't help but worry that I will eventually take my mother's place, and my sons will experience this pain. However, I am not going to start smelling peanut butter or staring at flashing lights—well, not yet anyway.

I am emotionally spent. The hospice nurse told me early in the day that her passing could happen at any time. Just as the body knows how to be born, the body knows how to die. Mom had stopped urinating. The nurse told me that this is evidence that her body is shutting down. We stop taking in fluids. Our body stops excreting them. Toxins build. Once this happens, you are close to death. It is a heart-wrenching exercise, particularly with Alzheimer's. At a certain point the miracles of modern medicine can save the physical body of your loved one through antibiotics, fluids, and other things, but his/her/their mind has gone. For many moments, I wondered whether the physicality would be enough, but at least in my case, this is unfair to my loved one—a person who was full of opinions, life, ideas, and desires. However, more than once, I have wanted to return to the in-between state: a state in which Mom recognized me but was not her entire self.

The hospice nurse then informed me that sometimes people wait to pass until their loved ones leave. At that exact moment, Mom raised her right hand. It was an odd, startling gesture for someone who has had little movement. The nurse and I stared at each other—we started laughing—finally, a moment of levity! "Maybe she wants you to leave," said the nurse. I tried to give Mom a hug and a kiss on the cheek before I left—I wanted a hug so badly. Even a one-way hug. She recoiled with a look of disgust. It wasn't her fault. It didn't mean anything. It still stung. Alzheimer's. So cruel. Of course, she recoiled. I get it. *Who was I?* She had no idea. A stranger had entered her room and tried to grab her. In her warped reality, recoiling was a completely appropriate reaction. Even from her own daughter.

I was afraid to return. But there she was, alive. I made a promise to Liz when she first began helping Mom. The promise was that even if Liz were no longer helping Mom, she would be able to see her before death. I texted Liz, and we video chatted with Mom. It was the best I could do in these COVID times. I believe that Mom recognized her voice. Her loud booming voice wishing Mom well. She is a preacher, literally, and told Mom about all the love the Lord had for her and what a wonderful journey she would take. Although I am not a very religious person, hearing her explanation and wishes brought me great peace.

I texted close relatives about her status and asked if they wanted to video chat. We had a nice call with family. Mom had been sleeping and sort of in and out of being awake, but certain voices prompted her to become completely alert with both eyes open, staring at the phone. There was still something going on inside that head! I wondered if she was trying to tell me to call people before. But then I remembered her doctor's words that she probably was not capable of that depth of thought. *Did the voice just sound familiar, and she liked the sound of it?*

My relatives thanked me profusely, but what they don't understand is that I see this as my duty. A promise I made to my parents. I am your legs. I get that you could not come. I know you wanted to. It would be horrible if you did travel, caught COVID, and brought it into this building, I tried to explain. It must have been so difficult for you not to come. I admire you immensely for the selflessness of not coming. This led to a call with other family members.

"We love you, Grandma Jane."

"You were a great mom, and I am so thankful for everything you taught me."

"Don't worry about us, Grandma Jane!"

"We are all okay."

Intimate calls before death etched into my brain. The one I can't forget that replays in my mind is: "Do whatever you need to do. We will be okay." Smiling, loving faces and voices.

Of course, in COVID times there was a lot of "Mary, can you move the camera? I can only see her forehead" and "Could you turn the camera around so that I can also see her?" or "I can only see part of her face." Lots of "Could you raise the volume?" and "You are on mute." It's like, of all the things to have to worry about. Really?! It reminded me of a contract negotiation I recently had where I was looking up our client's nostril during a three-hour video call because that was the only position where we could hear him clearly.

There is a famous antitrust case where the FBI used a lamp with a camera in it to record meetings.[1] As the story goes, the lamp took a worldwide tour of conference rooms. Lawyers used to wonder why no one noticed the lamp—because it was always the same lamp, but often did not match the decor. I felt like the lamp. The conduit of several most intimate conversations of which I should not have been a part. A necessary but misplaced fixture.

She brought me into this world. I am now assisting her in leaving it. It is hard being in her room alone, but I think of all the families who did not have this opportunity, and despite my sadness, I am thankful. I am thankful that I can be here with her. I am thankful for the building management who let me come and go as I wish. I am thankful for the hospice team. I am thankful for my smartphone that allowed Mom to see her children. I am thankful to Mom—she always did have impeccable timing.

As I walked back to her room from the restroom, I thought about the fact that I would no longer be coming here to visit her. I would no longer be allowed in the building. No longer saying hello on the weekends at the front desk. No more noodles. No more fifth floor access. No more walking by the restaurant downstairs. No more weird smell. No more swiping a piece of fruit from the mail area.

The home is on the way to the boys' school—*will I think about it every day? How many people have died on this floor?* There are so many empty rooms . . . they used to be all full. Names on every door. So many doors without names. *Was it COVID? Is this normal?* I haven't been able to go to the fifth floor since March. I feel comfortable here. I will no longer have a reason to come here. Someone else will live where she died—maybe she lives where someone else died. I feel lost.

I left at about 11:00 p.m. with Mom listening to piano music and a hint of lavender in the air from the air freshener I brought earlier in the week. She watched me without moving as I tucked her in with her sunflower blanket, just like I used to tuck in my children: "Tuck, tuck, tuck . . . and don't forget the feet!" I left wondering if I should stay.

In the lobby before I left a Pal stopped me and asked if I were coming back that evening. "No," I said, "not until tomorrow." She was glad. She apologized for being glad, but apparently there was a list of people who wanted to say goodbye to Jane but did not want to disturb me out of respect. She ran through the list. There were at least ten people. There was an agreed order. A line. Multiple conversations had occurred. The thought of a line of people who cared for my mother—all wanting to say goodbye—made me sad, but simultaneously, it was the first time I felt good about leaving her to go home. They should have that opportunity. Even with Alzheimer's, Mom had a life. She should hear from all her friends. I hoped they would all be able to tell Mom how much they cared. I appreciated their waiting until I left, although they were certainly welcome while I remained, and I appreciated the feelings they had for my mother. Mom should receive all the love she can before she leaves us for whatever is next. The thought of all the genuine love and good wishes Mom was about to receive felt like I was also under her warm sunflower blanket.

Sunday, November 29, 2020

I woke up very early for a Sunday with a depth of sadness I had never experienced. It was around seven in the morning. I woke up my older son and told him I was leaving to see Grandma Jane. "So early on a Sunday?"

I decided to treat myself and stop for coffee along the way. When my latte and I returned to the car, a Pal called my cell phone. "Hi! I am on my way—there in two minutes!"

"Oh . . . they haven't called you yet?"

It had happened.

The hospice doctor had said the best-case scenario would be to walk into Mom's room one morning and see that she had passed peacefully in her sleep. A good death, apparently. Well, it seems she had a good death.

I was in my car in front of the coffee shop. Alone with my latte, all I could think was, *Your mother has died. You have no living parents. You know this information. Your brothers do not. Mom's siblings do not. They think she is alive, but she is dead.*

I did not know what to do or where to go. The thought of returning home felt like defeat. I would also have to explain why I had returned, and I was not ready to speak this news out loud. If no one in our family knows, maybe she still lives in some weird way. I wanted to go to the fifth floor. I wanted to say goodbye. I wanted to see her. I convinced myself that the information must be incorrect. No doctor had called me, just a Pal. No one from the hospice company had called. So, I resumed my plan and finished the drive to her nursing facility. I had this uncontrollable desire to be with her. Stopping at Starbucks seems so trivial and stupid now.

I arrived and took the elevator to the fifth floor, opened the fifth-floor door with the secret code, and walked to her room. There she was in her bed. It seemed the information was correct. I won't describe how the human body looks when someone has passed. It's not bad, honestly; it's just different. You see your loved one, but it's clearly just their body. They look like themselves, but their soul has left. They look as if there is no longer life. Their body is the shell of a cicada. Flashbacks to my father in his deathbed flew through my head. They both died "a good death," but how can any death from Alzheimer's complications ever be "good"?

This morning was so surreal. Mom dead in her room still with piano music playing and hints of lavender, and life at her nursing home continuing around her. Her sunflower blanket just as I left it last night. Tuck, tuck, tuck, just like my kids. *At what time did she pass? Was it just after I left? Should I have stayed? Would she have had the moment of lucidity?* No, I should not have stayed. Mom had a life. Friends. I assume people were able to say goodbye. Answers to questions I will never know. I touched her shoulder and told her I loved her—maybe she is still warm. But she felt exactly like my father when I touched his shoulder. I hope they are together in some way. I closed my eyes tightly and waited for some type of sign or feeling from God or the universe or whatever—just wanting to know what happens after death . . . nothing. I said a prayer and stepped out into the hallway.

A Pal I knew walked over to me in the hallway, declared she was breaking the COVID rules, and gave me a huge hug. The first hug in so many months. I could hear the piano music in the background. A neighbor struggling with his walker was leaving his room to go to breakfast. "Don't tell Jimmy!" he blurted out.

The Pal responded immediately, "Okay, I won't tell Jimmy a thing!"

Another person across the hall came out of her room in her wheelchair—"I feel good today!"

"That's great!" replied the Pal.

I was standing in the hallway in shock. I watched Mom's neighbors as they slowly traveled down the hall. Signs of life with death also present.

WEED

By Jane P. Moreland

Two warm days break through winter, and the weed
is up and waving lime shamrocks around bricks
and stepping stones, snaking roots through mulch
to intrude on pansies, free at last from the tight fists
of tiny bulbs. It bothers me. I launch digging wars
with gloved hands, trace roots through dark soil,
spray herbicides, but still it multiplies.

I remember from childhood the sour taste
of its stringy stems, how it ran rife in our yard,
how Mother started spring with a trowel, moved
to butcher knives, then despaired until its decline
in winter's dark days. Later, it traveled unseen
from her yard to mine in clumps and root balls
dug at dawn and piled into the trunk of her car.

I never knew its name until one Easter late
in her life. We sat on my lawn as children found eggs,
and the weed bloomed in every pot and bed.
I asked its name and heard three distant syllables
squeezed low into her throat, faraway notes rising
as if through the tapered horn of her old Victrola,
then released into air: "Oxalis."

Oxalis arrives anew every spring, weaving
its leaves among violets and jade succulents,
circling new sprouts of grape hyacinths and tulips
and then suddenly blooming in the tiny pink trumpets
I have come to know as my mother's lingering words,
for at the sight of those blooms, I hear
in that gravelly, waning voice, "I am near."

Chapter 13

When Caregiving Ends

I have been looking at pictures all morning. Comparing the pictures to one I swiped from Mom's room of her and my dad on the way out. I see how much she had deteriorated. To me, it was a slow, bit-by-bit deterioration, and I was happy for every little salvageable bit of my mother. It was her time, I know, but selfishly, there was comfort for me in visiting her and knowing she was still around. I see objectively that she had no life—she would not have wanted to live this way. But I just liked being around her, even if she had no idea who I was. I moved her just down the street from me so that I could hop on over any time I liked.

Honestly, I liked taking care of her. I often felt overwhelmed, but I loved her so. I felt needed. I was important. Being a caregiver of my children and my mother has defined me. It has been my main purpose in life. I was the meat of the sandwich. I did important things.

I went to the store to get dinner for my kids, and I automatically thought, *Okay, is there anything Mom needs?* I was her primary caregiver for close to a decade. I was part of the sandwich generation—now I am no longer. There is no open-faced sandwich generation. Just like that, I am no longer in the sandwich generation. I am now just a single parent with teenage kids who are going off to college in a couple of years. Other generations are for life: baby boomers, Generation X, millennials, Generation Z. The sandwich generation defines you until it does not. I worried about her. All the time. She was my third child—not the mother in my youth, but Jane who had Alzheimer's was my child. I am still worrying about her—she is gone. *How do I stop worrying? What is my life?*

What is the relationship I had with my mother? There were several. *What is my relationship with Mom, Grandma Jane, Jane, Baby Jane?* They are all my mother.

I am concerned for myself. This was part of my identity; I took care of all matters "Mom." I feel lost. Her room was the last little bit of my former life—the painting of Mexican fishing boats above her bed, the pictures of baby grandchildren who are now adults, the monarch butterfly needlepoint pillows she made, the sunflower blanket I wrapped myself in for the last few days while sitting in the salmon-colored chair until I tucked her into her bed. It was a safe place from the past. Now I will need to dismantle it just like I did their home. The final goodbye of my youth. It's just all gone except for the memories in my head.

Mom was my purpose. She was as important to me as my children. Everyone else went on with life—a visit, a lunch with Jane . . . but she was my *purpose*. My goal was to care for her, to make her happy and comfortable. To make sure she had what she needed. I felt good being the caretaker. I love taking care of others. It just fits.

It's gone. I miss her so much, and it's over. At times I resented the responsibility, but then I would remember the trust placed in me and be appreciative for the love it took to put a child in charge of your life and well-being. What a compliment. I am floored. However, I need some skills for how to move forward. The training may have included *this is what we want, here is what is important to me,* but it did not include how you deal with life after being responsible for another. *How do I take care of myself?* I don't think I have those skills . . . yet. I must and will acquire them.

I think I mourned each loss of her abilities, but never the loss of the whole person. Looking at pictures I had forgotten what she really looked like. She was so elegant and beautiful. Always so put together. Lipstick, hair, clothes. So stylish. I think initially I was sad for everything she could no longer do, but at the end I was so thankful for anything she could do—including when she made eye contact with me. I wish I had looked at more pictures throughout her disease—to remember how she was. I had forgotten. I was just so in the day-to-day of life that I never looked at the big picture and appreciated *all* of the changes. Maybe this is why I feel so bad.

I remember the last school event she attended, the way people reacted to her. Her obvious discomfort. I thought maybe at the end she would have a moment of lucidity, but of course she did not. Her doctor told me she would not, but I just did not accept it.

I see that it was her time, but I just feel so sad, angry at the disease, and just like I want to go back in time. I want my mom—but how silly; for eight and a half years I have been watching her slip away. Of course, she is not there. Some of those years just seem like a blur. *Did I do the best I could?* She should have had an organized closet and a color-coded wardrobe. I was so sad about the limitations early on, but now that I have seen the end—those were the good times. I wish I had appreciated them more. I wish I had appreciated her more. Before she died, I thanked her for everything. Since I was the lamp, I heard many others thank her too. *Why didn't we thank her earlier?* Maybe they did, but I did not.

I read and was told by learned people—priests and psychiatrists— that typically when the person living with dementia passes, family members feel a sense of relief. By this time, the family has witnessed the long deterioration of the person they once loved and is relieved for that person to be in a better place. I waited for my sense of relief, but all I felt was sadness, anger, and loss. *Where is my sense of relief?* I was counting on the sense of relief! It is nowhere. I want my sense of relief, dammit! Not only did Alzheimer's rob me of a sense of lucidity before passing, it seems there is also no sense of relief—Alzheimer's stole that too. Alzheimer's is a thief.

I read in my books how people felt the person at the end was not the person before the disease. But I never thought that; she was always my mother. Her essence was always the same. She was just ill. That was not her fault. She wasn't exactly my mother, but she was in there somewhere, I thought. She had the same elegant hands. She was the same physical person. Or maybe the changes happened so gradually that I just lost my perspective. Or maybe I just did not want to see it. I have watched this— participated in it—for close to a decade, *so why am I so shocked?*

No more sandwich generation—just like that. One side of bread is gone. The other is being eaten away and soon will be gone. There is no open-faced sandwich generation. There is no meat generation. The list of things to do is shorter. Maybe that's the relief people refer to. *Is it/ was it selfish to want her around, even though she would have no quality of life, just so I could go and visit her?* It is understandable, but I think it is selfish. It is true—she would not have wanted to continue living as she was. I just want my mom back like she was in my pictures. That person has been gone for a while, but I always hoped she would reappear at least for a few minutes. Early in her disease I could get her back with enough effort (or at least I thought I could), but that ability went away a long time ago.

For several months Mom was in and out of hospitals and skilled facilities, and I was prohibited from visiting her. During that time, I forgot to cancel her deliveries of personal supplies, resulting in months' worth of underwear and sanitary wipes. Mountains of "female underwear" stuffed in cabinets, closets, and pushed under furniture. After her death I had planned to donate the underwear and supplies to the Salvation Army with some of her other things, when I saw a (relatively) younger woman walking her husband down the hallway. She stopped me and asked if I was moving in. I explained about my mother's passing. Her husband had recently moved to the fifth floor due to his early-onset dementia. We shared a tender moment, and I asked if she would like any supplies— although, since my mother was female, and her husband was male and quite taller, I wasn't sure what would be useful for him. She said she would like to come by the room and look.

I was afraid she would judge me for the excess of mountains of underwear and supplies, but she looked pensively at all of it and said, "I'll take it all. All of it. Whatever you don't want I will take it." I thought she would want only unopened packages due to COVID—but I was wrong. She wanted all of it. Opened and unopened. Half-used shampoo. Lotion.

Soap. Diapers. Wipes. Toothpaste. With a tear in her eye, she told me that this was the best Christmas gift she had ever received. She confided that she had not appreciated all the extra costs beyond the cost of the room. I did not know if I should feel happy or sad, but I was glad Jane's kind spirit lived on . . . even if only in underwear.

Today, for some reason, I started wondering: *What would Mom want me to do with my life going forward? What are my priorities?* My days are limited. *How should I use them?*

After my mom passed away, I posted a Facebook message about her death. A friend of mine responded—"Nobody loves you like your momma." If you are lucky enough to have an excellent momma, how true. My mother listened and empathized with me about everything and nothing. I know I should be happy for my mom. Many people do not experience the unconditional love of a mother. I am lucky, but it still hurts.

It still makes me mad that Mom was diagnosed with Alzheimer's, a disease that will probably have a cure in the next fifty years. It still makes me mad that Mom literally did everything suggested to prevent Alzheimer's and still had Alzheimer's. It makes me mad that she lifted weights every day, rode a bike, put flax on her cereal, and still died of Alzheimer's. She wrote poetry, attended classes, exercised her brain, and still died of Alzheimer's. She had no belly fat in her fifties.

I am between the stages of wanting to yell and cry because, apart from the slow loss of my mom, I believe that I will probably also eventually be diagnosed with Alzheimer's. I think of how I can prepare my children for this loss. The only consolation I have is that I can talk to my children about Alzheimer's now and tell them how I would like for them to live their lives, and that, as the victim of Alzheimer's, I probably will not realize what I have lost. I can provide them with the gift of documentation. I can tell them to enjoy their life and try to impart wisdom. I can try to instill a sense of self-confidence and encourage my two sons to always support each other. I can plan financially for my eventual care. While I imagine these things should bring me solace, they just make everything worse. However, at the same time, it is a reminder to live each day. Go for it! My dear friend sent me a thought of the day recently: "In the end, we only regret the chances we didn't take."

Tomorrow is Mother's Day.

My friend asked me for a favor: to facilitate the purchase of a gift for her daughter-in-law who lives in town. She just gave birth to her first child. Of course, I was happy to oblige. Manicure and pedicure, we decided, at my neighborhood salon where we had been together. Flowers and a card. I would sign the gift card from her and her husband and deliver it to her daughter-in-law.

As I looked through the cards at the store, it struck me. There were so many kind messages to mothers in the cards. "I love you, Mom." "I appreciate all you do for me." "You are my best friend, Mom." "Mom, you have taught me so much." Behind my COVID mask I felt loss. Such a huge loss. My mother was here last year—in 2020—but not in 2021. Flashes of my youth ran through my brain. Mother's Day lunches when I was a child. Flowers for Mom. Calling my mom when I was in college and lived in New York to wish her a happy Mother's Day. Sending her a Mother's Day surprise in the mail. Visiting my mother when I moved back to Houston. *Happy Mother's Day.*

However, I realized that the last several Mother's Days had, to be gentle, not been ideal. My mother had not recognized me. She was confined to a wheelchair. She was generally silent. However, she was still my mom. She was still there, although she was not. I could still celebrate Mother's Day with my mom. Thinking back a bit further, I recall a Mother's Day in 2011 when my father did not want to have lunch. "We will just stay home this year," he told me. *Was she ill? Did he know? Was he ill?* At the time I thought it was me and wondered why they were upset with me, but in retrospect I think it was something else. Something private he did not want me to know.

As I looked through the cards my eyes welled with tears. Not for the mom with dementia, but for the mom of my youth. I wished I had squeezed her tight and told her how much I loved her, as I do with my children—even though they are now teenagers, and I sometimes see them brace themselves for the inevitable hug. I regretted every teenage argument. If only I could will her back and tell her how much I admired her. And then I wondered how my mother felt about her mother. *Did she feel the same? Did my grandmother feel the same?* I wondered about all of the mothers of my life. *Is this a "repeatable offense"? Do all the moms leave with things unsaid? Do all the daughters survive with things to say?*

Sometimes the most ordinary things make me think of Mom, and I miss her wholeheartedly. I jump into the photograph of my youth and live as if my mother were still with me. I was at work one day when a text message with a picture dinged on my phone. My son in a kennel with a dog named Simba. For quite a while I had longed for the companionship of a dog. My kids were getting older, and despite my status as caretaker of two children and Jane, and my busy work and travel schedule, I missed having someone who would not leave my side.

True to our Generation Z household, all major household decisions were discussed and voted upon. My older son, an early teenager, told me we were too irresponsible for a dog—we would have to feed the dog, walk the dog, train the dog, play with the dog, and take the dog to the vet. We cannot handle it, he decreed. My younger son preferred cats. My reminding them that I had raised the two of them and had been a single parent since they were toddlers fell on deaf ears. "You are human! You require much more than a dog!" I said. No, Mom. Two votes to one. No dog.

I recalled when my parents kept Mr. Izzy, a miniature bulldog, the first child of my ex-husband and myself, while we were on vacation. When I returned, my father immediately pulled me aside into the study to inform me that my husband and I were always welcome, but Mr. Izzy was not. Stunned, I looked for my mother. "Oh, Mr. Izzy, quite the handful! Here is where he scratched a hole in the dry wall, but that's okay, I am sure I can repair it. Mr. Izzy scratched the paint off of the door, but what is paint? We can color match." She was so nice. I guess she knew how awful

I would feel and did not need to explain how angry she was. Or perhaps it was just passive-aggressiveness. Whichever it was, it worked. Maybe the guys were right.

Simba had been taken away from his family by another family member. He was thin and skittish. Someone had obviously shaved off his matted fur in a scraggly and uneven haircut. He walked around in the house in circles, looking nervously at us in the living room as he passed hastily. A real doggy Prozac candidate. He pranced like a deer when he ran. When he finally was given a dog toy, he punched it with his snout on the floor. When he heard the squeak, he would stare at the toy in shock. He huffed at me in despair when our cat, Newspaper, lounged in front of a doorway he wanted to enter or sat in his favorite chair staring down at him with full knowledge of his cat superiority.

Simba eventually gained confidence. No longer between his legs, his tail rose in the air like a cheerleader's happy pom-pom. Dog toys squeaked as he bit them. The cat accepted him as an inferior being. He developed a fondness for cat toys. My son became a responsible dog dad. Simba met two other dogs in the neighborhood, and we walked with his friends regularly. All was perfect, but for Simba's secret leash aggression.

Initially, I was able to hide the leash aggression by saying things like, "That's how he says hello!" or hiding behind cars or large trees during our walks while other dogs passed with their humans. For a while this worked; however, eventually Simba started barking several houses before the house with a dog. He caught on to my car and tree trickery. When we met a dog—even a cute toy dog—he would act nice, luring it to him until they were just inches apart, and then become aggressive. Usually calm with his walking buddies, Simba could no longer hide his desires. Our doggy friend's parents suggested a dog trainer and texted me the details. We were welcome in the backyard, but no longer on walks. Simba was a bad influence. Something must be done. I called the dog trainer.

She arrived at our house with an orange shirt stamped "Dog Counselor" and a purple rope leash wrapped around her chest like an intricate scarf or a girl scout badge sash. She was more of a behavioralist than an obedience trainer, she explained. Simba needed to see me as a mother figure. I needed to set structure with rules. When he wants to go in the backyard, I must provide permission to do so. When he wants to eat, he must sit until I allow it. I needed to repeatedly provide positive affirmation for anything and everything. Simba was a toddler. He needed the same structure, rules, and guidance as a happy human toddler. Although her rules and suggestions felt odd, particularly the one about sniffing the grass together, I admit that her advice and guidance worked marvelously. Doggy counselor is she!

As I walked Simba around the block today, I must have repeated "good boy, good Simba, good walk" fifty times, and I could not help but miss my mother. She would have gotten such a kick out of the training. She would have walked with me and chimed in occasionally with a "good boy" to be supportive and then laughed privately. She would have listened, feigning interest as I explained Simba's leash aggression. She would have howled internally at the idea of me hiding behind cars or trees to avoid other pets and hiring the Dog Counselor. She would have tried to keep her laughter to herself, but without success. I would have been slightly offended but joined in her laughter. We would have talked about childhood pets and Mr. Izzy's destruction.

Mom was different than Jane, but Jane would have listened as well. She would not have understood, but she would have smiled when I smiled and laughed when I laughed. She would have enjoyed the walk. I would have attributed more understanding to her smiles and laughs. She would have known that her daughter Mary or The Nice Lady was telling her something, and she would have been happy to see Mary or The Nice Lady laugh, which would make her in turn happy.

Baby Jane would not be able to go on the walk. She would listen and stare at me as I told her the story but show no emotion. However, I believe she would be happy internally for the positive energy. I believe that Baby Jane felt a closeness when I was around. She would stare into your eyes and you into hers, hoping for a connection or show of emotion. You would feel a connection with her locking eyes and wonder if she did as well. You would be happy that you held eye contact, waiting for some type of signal. You would agree that just being with someone you love is sometimes enough. You would hold her hand, the same elegant hands you had always known.

Afterword

Despite all advice to the contrary, I was convinced that my mother would miraculously reappear on her deathbed. I fantasized how in her final moments she would recognize me, and I would tell her how much I loved her. I believed that she would have a final moment of lucidity, perhaps a gift from God, that would reunite us. I would look into her eyes, into her soul, and she into mine. We would hug each other tightly, and she would tell me not to worry because we would be reunited and see each other again. I would tell her she was just fine, and she would assure me I was as well. Frequently when I was upset about her descent, I consoled myself by thinking that we would see each other again in her final moments, and I would have the opportunity to tell her the things I was always too busy to say and too preoccupied to think of.

As you know now, this did not happen. Alzheimer's takes away and never returns. Your loved one slowly leaves. It is a crushing experience to witness. I have cried rivers and lakes watching my mother slip away. I long for the days when we talked, shared, and laughed. I imagine us sitting in the living room chatting and giggling. Such a simple activity that I took for granted and never questioned the gift of being able to do so. I wish I had spent more time appreciating what was there, rather than mourning what was not.

I think every child of an Alzheimer's parent fears he or she will meet the same fate, and our children will experience our own slow descent. Simple things like a connection with a friend, the love of a pet, a board game, sharing a long meal, listening to my children talk about their experiences at school are important. Once it's over, it's over. The fact that I may have solved a legal issue, assisted in winning a bid or met a deadline is not as important as giggling in the living room or taking a vacation with a friend. I used to not feel this way; my life was measured through goals achieved. Maybe I have aged. Perhaps this is part of growing old. However, starting today, balance will be the priority, not just a goal.

Until today, balance in life has been a goal, but not the priority. As a lawyer, I was fortunate to work from home during the pandemic. Working from home eliminated the one-and-a-half-hour commute and led to a more flexible schedule, which allowed me to fill that time with dog walking, cooking, school commuting, and being present with my children. I have realized that—at least for myself—walking the dog, exercising, and being present in the moment is just as important (if not more so) as taking the conference call or reviewing the contract. These are things I have done for myself, not for the company and not for my paycheck.

My son is learning how to drive and has been driving us to school for practice. This morning while he drove, and NPR droned in the background, I thought about how I would feel if today were my last day. *Would I have accomplished what I wanted in life? What would please me about my life? What would I regret? What would I regret not doing? Have I prepared my children? Have I taught them all I can? Are they ready to live a life without me?*

So many people have died during COVID. Young people, old people, middle-aged people. I have a younger friend who was on a ventilator for two weeks. She sent me a text early in the pandemic: "There are no second chances." I knew a lawyer my age who died of COVID, a former co-worker. I wondered what he was doing before he became ill. I make up that he was moving words around and making edits on a piece of paper called a contract that he probably did not really care about. Just another contract to review. Perhaps that's completely incorrect, but it is a very possible scenario. How depressing.

Each day is a gift. *How am I using that gift?* Life is finite. Children grow up and have their own lives. Our jobs as parents are to prepare them for that life. Seasons change. Life continues after the death of a loved one. Living in the past and yearning for a former life or person will not move you forward to a new fulfilling life. At some point, a break must be made even though you would prefer to keep it together with duct tape or superglue.

In *The Year of Magical Thinking*, Joan Didion writes, "I know why we try to keep the dead alive: we try to keep them alive in order to keep them with us. I also know that if we are to live ourselves there comes a point at which we must relinquish the dead, let them go, keep them dead. Let them become the photograph on the table."[1]

I don't want my loved ones to remain in the photograph; I want them here with me. I don't want to forget the sound of my mother's voice, the feel of her hugs, or the inevitable whiff of Oil of Olay while hugging my grandmother. I don't want to forget that holiday celebrations were full of relatives, multiple cakes and pies and East Texas desserts I never liked. I want to return to the room on the fifth floor where my mother and I stared into each other's eyes. I want to return to the restaurant in San Antonio when we wore ponchos and ordered coffee. I want to return to the trip to New Orleans to find an apartment before law school. I want to hold her elegant hands. I want to giggle with her about nothing.

I want to be in the photograph. I do not have to forget these experiences that I want, but for the progression of my own life and the well-being of my children, I need to let these memories remain in the photo album. New memories must be made. New photographs taken. It takes a conscious effort for me to not live in the photograph with people I have loved and still love, but I must remind myself that there are new and happy photographs that await. For the sake of myself, I must train my mind to leave my past and walk out of the photo. I must accept the fact that my mother, father, grandparents, friends, and others belong in the photograph and would not want me in it with them. I must become uncomfortable and face the unknown future without the people I love. I must take the initiative however uncomfortable and make new photographs. I must make new photographs, even if I am struggling to smile in them at first.

Last night I had a dream. I was in my parents' bedroom of our family home. It was empty, just like I left it before it sold. They were both there.

There was my mother. "Hi, Mare." She knew who I was. I hugged her. It felt so real. "Mom! I'm just so happy to see you!" and then I would step back, look at her in disbelief and hug her again. "I'm just so happy you are here, and with Dad too!"

"Mom, do you know who I am?" I asked my mother.

"Yes, Mare. Of course, I know who you are," she would scoff and roll her eyes, a bit annoyed.

"Really?!" I would hug her again. I did this about five times. She was thin again—she looked like herself. A little out of it, but she knew what was generally going on around her. I felt the hug. In my dream, I felt it. I felt her bones. It was familiar. I felt her skin. It was *so* familiar. I could almost smell Chanel No. 5.

We were in our family home: it was empty but just as it was. We were in their bedroom—except that my mother's closet was partially full. This was their dream home. They designed it, lived there forty years. The navy, coffee stained, and ripped-up carpet was still there.

My father walked in and said, "This is just too upsetting for me—I had not seen the house empty like this." He left and told me to help Mom get packed. They needed to go. He had a sense of urgency about him. All business.

"Well, what clothes do I need?" she asked.

"You don't need anything fancy, but you need more than what you have on now." She was either in a robe or hospital gown, I don't quite remember. But I do remember that she was standing on her own and looking at me, her daughter whom she recognized—Mare—for help packing for her trip, and exasperated with her husband for the lack of clarity in packing instructions.

In Mom's closet there were Dad's suits and some of Mom's clothes—I touched a suit. It was gray. "Do you need a suit?" I asked.

"No. No suits."

"Come on, Mare," my dad urged, "get her packed."

I can't describe the feeling I felt when I woke up. I experienced this feeling of pure, clean happiness—it was wonderful, but then I realized it was just a dream.

It made me remember another dream. Shortly after my dad died, I had a dream where I sat on a park bench. He appeared and sat behind me on another bench. We were sitting back-to-back on two park benches facing opposite directions.

"Dad, why did you leave?"

"It was my time to go."

"But I need you here. I am not ready for this."

"Mare, everything is going to be okay."

"But I wasn't ready for you to go. I need you here."

"It was my time, Mare."

And then he left, and I turned to look at him. He walked off. He had no limp. No bad knee. No breathing equipment. He never looked back, but he jumped and clicked his heels together like in a 1950s movie as in my youth and walked away.

I was alone on the bench, but happy to have seen him so fit, glad that he had come to see me, wondering if he would get to see his own parents, and hoping we would see each other again.

The mind plays nasty tricks. Or maybe the mind helps us see what we want. Or maybe this was my parents reaching out to me, which is what I so desperately wanted. I think I will choose what I would like for it to be, just as I will choose what I will do in this next stage of my life.

Chapter 1

1. Alzheimer's Association, *2021 Alzheimer's Disease Facts and Figures* (Chicago, IL: Alzheimer's Association, 2021), https://www.alz.org/media/Documents/alzheimers-facts-and-figures.pdf.

2. Ibid.

3. "What is Alzheimer's Disease?" Alzheimer's Association, accessed November 22, 2021, https://www.alz.org/alzheimers-dementia/what-is-alzheimers.

4. Ibid.

5. "2021 Alzheimer's Disease Facts and Figures." Infographic. Alzheimer's Association, 2021. https://www.alz.org/media/Documents/alzheimers-facts-and-figures-infographic.pdf.

6. Alzheimer's Association, *2021 Alzheimer's Disease Facts and Figures* (Chicago, IL: Alzheimer's Association, 2021), https://www.alz.org/media/Documents/alzheimers-facts-and-figures.pdf.

7. "Dementia," World Health Organization, last modified September 2, 2021, https://www.who.int/en/news-room/fact-sheets/detail/dementia Dementia (who.int).

8. "Dementia facts & figures," Alzheimer's Disease International, accessed November 22, 2021, https://www.alzint.org/about/dementia-facts-figures/.

9. Alzheimer's Association, *2021 Alzheimer's Disease Facts and Figures* (Chicago, IL: Alzheimer's Association, 2021), https://www.alz.org/media/Documents/alzheimers-facts-and-figures.pdf.

10. Alzheimer's Association, *2021 Alzheimer's Disease Facts and Figures* (Chicago, IL: Alzheimer's Association, 2021), 8, figure 1, https://www.alz.org/media/Documents/alzheimers-facts-and-figures.pdf.

11. Alzheimer's Association, *2021 Alzheimer's Disease Facts and Figures* (Chicago, IL: Alzheimer's Association, 2021), https://www.alz.org/media/Documents/alzheimers-facts-and-figures.pdf.

12. Ibid.
13. Ibid.
14. Ibid.
15. Alzheimer's Society, *Caring for a person with dementia: A practical guide* (London, England: Alzheimer's Society, 2021), https://www.alzheimers. org.uk/sites/default/files/2020-03/caring_for_a_person_with_dementia_600.pdf.
16. Alzheimer's Association, *2021 Alzheimer's Disease Facts and Figures* (Chicago, IL: Alzheimer's Association, 2021), https://www.alz.org/media/Documents/alzheimers-facts-and-figures.pdf.
17. Ibid.
18. Ibid.
19. Ibid.
20. Alzheimer's Society, *Caring for a person with dementia: A practical guide* (London, England: Alzheimer's Society, 2021), https://www.alzheimers. org.uk/sites/default/files/2020-03/caring_for_a_person_with_dementia_600.pdf.
21. Alzheimer's Association, *2021 Alzheimer's Disease Facts and Figures* (Chicago, IL: Alzheimer's Association, 2021), https://www.alz.org/media/Documents/alzheimers-facts-and-figures.pdf.
22. Ibid.
23. Alzheimer's Society, *Caring for a person with dementia: A practical guide* (London, England: Alzheimer's Society, 2021), https://www.alzheimers. org.uk/sites/default/files/2020-03/caring_for_a_person_with_dementia_600.pdf.
24. Alzheimer's Association, *2021 Alzheimer's Disease Facts and Figures* (Chicago, IL: Alzheimer's Association, 2021), https://www.alz.org/media/Documents/alzheimers-facts-and-figures.pdf.
25. Ibid.
26. Alzheimer's Society, *Caring for a person with dementia: A practical guide* (London, England: Alzheimer's Society, 2021), https://www.alzheimers. org.uk/sites/default/files/2020-03/caring_for_a_person_with_dementia_600.pdf.
27. Alzheimer's Association, *2021 Alzheimer's Disease Facts and Figures* (Chicago, IL: Alzheimer's Association, 2021), https://www.alz.org/media/Documents/alzheimers-facts-and-figures.pdf.; Alzheimer's Society, *Caring for a person with dementia: A practical guide* (London, England: Alzheimer's Society, 2021), https://www.alzheimers.org.uk/sites/default/files/2020-03/caring_for_a_person_with_dementia_600.pdf.

Chapter 2

1. CPR & First Aid Emergency Cardiovascular Care. 2021. "What is CPR." American Heart Association, accessed November 23, 2021, https://cpr. heart.org/en/resources/what-is-cpr.
2. American Heart Association. 2019. "CPR Statistics." American Heart Association, accessed November 23, 2021, https://cprblog.heart.org/ cpr-statistics/.
3. Ibid.

Chapter 3

1. AlzConnected (*website*). Alzheimer's Association, 2021, accessed November 23, 2021, https://www.alzconnected.org/default.aspx.
2. "Suspicions and Delusions." Alzheimer's Association. Accessed November 23, 2021, https://www.alz.org/help-support/caregiving/stages-behaviors/ suspicions-delusions.
3. "Communication (for dementia)." Family Caregiver Alliance, accessed November 23, 2021, https://www.caregiver.org/resource/ communication-dementia/?via=caregiver-resources,caring-for-another,be-havior-management-strategies.
4. "Communication and Alzheimer's." Alzheimer's Association, accessed November 23, 2021, https://www.alz.org/help-support/caregiving/ daily-care/communications.
5. Ibid.
6. Ibid.
7. "Alzheimer's and dementia: Tips for better communication." Healthy Lifestyle Caregivers, Mayo Clinic, March 12, 2021. https://www.mayoc-linic.org/healthy-lifestyle/caregivers/in-depth/alzheimers/art-20047540.
8. "Communication and Alzheimer's." Alzheimer's Association, accessed November 23, 2021, https://www.alz.org/help-support/caregiving/ daily-care/communications.

Chapter 4

1. "50 Activities." Alzheimer's Association, accessed November 23, 2021, https://www.alz.org/help-support/resources/kids-teens/50-activities=.
2. "How to talk about dementia with children and young people." Alzheimer's Society, accessed November 23, 2021, https://www.alzheimers.org.uk/get-support/daily-living/ how-talk-dementia-children-young-people.

3. Alzheimer's Society. "Lasting power of Attorney and Dementia." November 19, 2021, *Youtube*, https://www.youtube.com/watch?v=9dtgLt4-Jaw.
4. "For Teens." Alzheimer's Association, accessed November 23, 2021, https://www.alz.org/help-support/resources/kids-teens/for_teens.

Chapter 5

1. "Getting Your Affairs in Order." National Institute on Aging, U.S. Department of Health and Human Services. Last reviewed June 1, 2018, https://www.nia.nih.gov/health/getting-your-affairs-order.
2. "CaringInfo." National Hospice and Palliative Care Organization, accessed November 23, 2021. https://www.caringinfo.org/planning/advance-directives/by-state/.
3. "Getting Your Affairs in Order." National Institute on Aging, U.S. Department of Health and Human Services. Last reviewed June 1, 2018, https://www.nia.nih.gov/health/getting-your-affairs-order.
4. Ibid.

Chapter 6

1. CareScout. *Genworth Cost of Care Survey: Summary and Methodology*. Genworth Cost of Care Surveys. New York: Genworth Financial Inc., 2020.
2. Alzheimer's Association. "2021 Alzheimer's Disease Facts and Figures." Infographic. Alzheimer's Association, 2021, https://www.alz.org/media/Documents/alzheimers-facts-and-figures-infographic.pdf.
3. "Care Options." Alzheimer's Association, accessed November 24, 2021, https://www.alz.org/help-support/caregiving/care-options.
4. "Creating Your Care Team." Alzheimer's Association, accessed November 24, 2021, https://www.alz.org/help-support/caregiving/care-options/care-team-calendar.
5. "Education Center." Alzheimer's Association, accessed November 24, 2021, https://training.alz.org/?5=page/1/page-size/25.
6. "essentiALZ®—Alzheimer's Association Training and Certification." Alzheimer's Association, accessed November 24, 2021, https://www.alz.org/professionals/professional-providers/dementia-care-training-certification/essentialz-training-program-certification.
7. "Caregiving." Home & Family, AARP, accessed November 24, 2021, https://www.aarp.org/home-family/caregiving/.

Chapter 7

1. "Driving Safety and Alzheimer's Disease." Alzheimer's Caregiving, National Institute on Aging, accessed November 24, 2021, https:// www.nia.nih.gov/health/driving-safety-and-alzheimers-disease#:~:text=When%20a%20person%20with%20Alzheimer%27s%20disease%20 is%20not,stop%20driving.%20Do%20this%20in%20a%20caring%20way.
2. "Learn More About Safe Senior Driving." California Department of Aging, State of California, accessed December 29, 2021, https://aging. ca.gov/How_Do_I/Learn_More_About_Safe_Senior_Driving/.
3. "Driving Safety and Alzheimer's Disease." Alzheimer's Caregiving, National Institute on Aging, accessed November 24, 2021, https:// www.nia.nih.gov/health/driving-safety-and-alzheimers-disease#:~:text=When%20a%20person%20with%20Alzheimer%27s%20disease%20 is%20not,stop%20driving.%20Do%20this%20in%20a%20caring%20 way.
4. Ibid.
5. "Traveling." Alzheimer's Association, accessed November 24, 2021. https://www.alz.org/help-support/caregiving/safetytraveling.

Chapter 8

1. "Sleep Issues and Sundowning." Alzheimer's Association, accessed November 24, 2021, https://www.alz.org/help-support/caregiving/ stages-behaviors/sleep-issues-sundowning.
2. Ibid.
3. Ibid.
4. "Alzheimer's Disease & Related Dementias." National Institute on Aging. US Department of Health & Human Services, accessed November 29, 2021, https://www.nia.nih.gov/health/alzheimers.; "Alzheimer's Home Page: National Institute on Aging." Alzheimers.gov, National Institute on Aging, National Institutes of Health, US Department of Health and Human services, accessed November 29, 2021, https://www.alzheimers.gov/.; "Caregiver Life Balance." Family Caregiving, AARP, accessed November 29, 2021, https://www.aarp.org/caregiving/life-balance/?migration=rdrct.; "Help and Support." Alzheimer's Association, accessed November 24, 2021, https://www.alz.org/help-support.; "Home." Family Caregiver Alliance, accessed November 29, 2021, https://www.caregiver.org/.
5. Drake, Tavé Fascé and Nikki Jardin. "Our Magazines—Mirador Magazine." *Mirador Magazine- Making Connections*, August 2021, https://www.miradormagazine.com/?page_id=1555.

Chapter 9

1. Donepezil (generic name for Aricept) is used to treat confusion (dementia) related to Alzheimer's disease. "Donepezil: MedlinePlus Drug Information." MedlinePlus, American Society of Health-System Pharmacists, Inc., last updated November 23, 2021, https://medlineplus.gov/druginfo/meds/a697032.html.
2. "50 Activities." Alzheimer's Association, accessed November 29, 2021, https://www.alz.org/help-support/resources/kids-teens/50-activities.
3. "Grief and Loss as Alzheimer's Progresses." Alzheimer's Association, accessed November 29, 2021, https://www.alz.org/help-support/caregiving/caregiver-health/grief-loss-as-alzheimers-progresses.
4. Ibid.

Chapter 11

1. "What is Palliative Care?" CaringInfo, National Hospice and Palliative Care Organization, accessed December 6, 2021, https://www.caringinfo.org/types-of-care/palliative-care/#where.
2. Ibid.
3. Alzheimer's Association, *Medicare's Hospice Benefit for Beneficiaries with Alzheimer's Disease*, (Chicago, IL: Alzheimer's Association, last updated March 2017), https://www.alz.org/national/documents/medicare_topicsheet_hospice_benefit.pdf#:~:text=Medicare%E2%80%99s%20hospice%20benefit%20for%20beneficiaries%20with.%20Alzheimer%27s%20disease,life%2C%20as%20well%20as%20physical%20care%20and%20counseling.
4. "Hospice Care." CaringInfo, National Hospice and Palliative Care Organization, accessed December 6, 2021, https://www.caringinfo.org/types-of-care/hospice-care/.
5. "Hospice Care." Medicare, US Centers for Medicare and Medicaid Services, accessed December 6, 2021, https://www.medicare.gov/coverage/hospice-care.
6. "How Hospice Works." Medicare, US Centers for Medicare and Medicaid Services, accessed December 6, 2021, https://www.medicare.gov/what-medicare-covers/what-part-a-covers/how-hospice-works.
7. "Hospice Care." Medicare, US Centers for Medicare and Medicaid Services, accessed December 6, 2021, https://www.medicare.gov/coverage/hospice-care; Alzheimer's Association, *Medicare's Hospice Benefit for Beneficiaries with Alzheimer's Disease*, (Chicago, IL: Alzheimer's Association, last updated March 2017), https://www.alz.org/national/

documents/medicare_topicsheet_hospice_benefit.pdf#:~:text=Medi-care%E2%80%99s%20hospice%20benefit%20for%20beneficiaries%20with.%20Alzheimer%27s%20disease,life%2C%20as%20well%20as%20physical%20care%20and%20counseling.

8. Alzheimer's Association, *Medicare's Hospice Benefit for Beneficiaries with Alzheimer's Disease*, (Chicago, IL: Alzheimer's Association, last updated March 2017), https://www.alz.org/national/documents/medicare_topicsheet_hospice_benefit.pdf#:~:text=Medi-care%E2%80%99s%20hospice%20benefit%20for%20beneficiaries%20with.%20Alzheimer%27s%20disease,life%2C%20as%20well%20as%20physical%20care%20and%20counseling.

9. Ibid.

Chapter 12

1. Hammond, Scott D. "Caught In The Act: Inside An International Cartel." The United States Department of Justice, October 18, 2005, https://www.justice.gov/atr/speech/caught-act-inside-international-cartel.

Afterword

1. Didion, Joan. *The Year of Magical Thinking*. New York City, New York: Knopf Doubleday Publishing Group, October 2005.

2021. AlzConnected (*website*). Alzheimer's Association,
https://www.alzconnected.org/default.aspx.

"50 Activities." Alzheimer's Association, accessed November 23, 2021,
https://www.alz.org/help-support/resources/kids-teens/50-activities.

Alzheimer's Association, *2021 Alzheimer's Disease Facts and Figures*
(Chicago, IL: Alzheimer's Association, 2021), https://www.alz.org/
media/Documents/alzheimers-facts- and-figures.pdf.

"Alzheimer's and dementia: Tips for better communication." Healthy Lifestyle
Caregivers, Mayo Clinic, March 12, 2021. https://www.mayoclinic.org/
healthy-lifestyle/caregivers/in-depth/alzheimers/art-20047540.

Alzheimer's Association. "2021 Alzheimer's Disease Facts and Figures."
Infographic. Alzheimer's Association, 2021, https://www.alz.org/media/
Documents/alzheimers-facts- and-figures-infographic.pdf.

Alzheimer's Association, *Medicare's Hospice Benefit for Beneficiaries with
Alzheimer's Disease*, (Chicago, IL.: Alzheimer's Association, last updated
March 2017), https://www.alz.org/national/documents/medicare_
topicsheet_hospice_benefit.pdf#:~:tex t=Medicare%E2%80%99s%20
hospice%20benefit%20for%20beneficiaries%20with.%20
Alzheimer%27s%20disease,life%2C%20as%20well%20as%20
physical%20care%20and %20counseling.

Alzheimer's Association, *Sundowning* (Chicago, IL: Alzheimer's Association,
December 2020), https://alz.org/media/Documents/alzheimers-dementia-
sundowning- ts.pdf#:~:text=Sundowning%20It%E2%80%99s%20common
%20for%20people%20livin g%20with%20Alzheimer%E2%80%99s,causing
%20more%20behavioral%20problems% 20late%20in%20the%20day.

"Alzheimer's Disease & Related Dementias." National Institute on Aging. US Department of Health & Human Services, accessed November 29, 2021, https://www.nia.nih.gov/health/alzheimers.

"Alzheimer's Home Page: National Institute on Aging." Alzheimers. gov, National Institute on Aging, National Institutes of Health, US Department of Health and Human services, accessed November 29, 2021, https://www.alzheimers.gov/.

Alzheimer's Society, *Caring for a person with dementia: A practical guide* (London, England: Alzheimer's Society, 2021), https://www.alzheimers. org.uk/sites/default/files/2020- 03/caring_for_a_person_with_ dementia_600.pdf.

Alzheimer's Society. "Lasting power of Attorney and Dementia." November 19, 2021, *YouTube*, https://www.youtube.com/watch?v=9dtgLt4-Jaw.

American Heart Association. 2019. "CPR Statistics." American Heart Association, accessed November 23, 2021, https://cprblog.heart.org/ cpr-statistics/.

"CaringInfo." National Hospice and Palliative Care Organization, accessed November 23, 2021. https://www.caringinfo.org/planning/ advance-directives/by-state/.

"Caregiver Life Balance." Family Caregiving, AARP, accessed November 29, 2021, https://www.aarp.org/caregiving/life-balance/?migration=rdrct.

"Caregiving." Home & Family, AARP, accessed November 24, 2021, https:// www.aarp.org/home-family/caregiving/.

CareScout. *Genworth Cost of Care Survey: Summary and Methodology*. Genworth Cost of Care Surveys. New York: Genworth Financial Inc., 2020.

"Care Options." Alzheimer's Association, accessed November 24, 2021, https://www.alz.org/help-support/caregiving/care-options.

Carter, Susi Singer and Don Priess. *Love Conquers Alz*, produced by Susi Singer Carter. 2019, Los Angeles: Go Girl Media. Podcast. https:// loveconquersalz.buzzsprout.com/.

Carter, Susi Singer, director. *My Mom and the Girl*. Go Girl Media, 2016. 20 min. https://www.imdb.com/title/tt5342718/fullcredits?ref_=tt_ov_st_sm

"Communication (for dementia)." Family Caregiver Alliance, accessed November 23, 2021, https://www.caregiver.org/resource/communication-dementia/?via=caregiver- resources,caring-for-another,behavior-management-strategies.

"Communication and Alzheimer's." Alzheimer's Association, accessed November 23, 2021, https://www.alz.org/help-support/caregiving/daily-care/communications.

CPR & First Aid Emergency Cardiovascular Care. 2021. "What is CPR." American Heart Association, accessed November 23, 2021, https://cpr.heart.org/en/resources/what-is-cpr.

"Creating Your Care Team." Alzheimer's Association, accessed November 24, 2021, https://www.alz.org/help-support/caregiving/care-options/care-team-calendar.

"Dementia," World Health Organization, last modified September 2, 2021, https://www.who.int/en/news-room/fact-sheets/detail/dementia Dementia (who.int).

"Dementia facts & figures," Alzheimer's Disease International, accessed November 22, 2021, https://www.alzint.org/about/dementia-facts-figures/.

Didion, Joan. *The Year of Magical Thinking*. New York City, New York: Knopf Doubleday Publishing Group, October 2005.

"Donepezil: MedlinePlus Drug Information." MedlinePlus, American Society of Health-System Pharmacists, Inc., last updated November 23, 2021, https://medlineplus.gov/druginfo/meds/a697032.html.

Drake, Tavé Fascé and Nikki Jardin. "Our Magazines – Mirador Magazine." *Mirador Magazine- Making Connections*, August 2021, https://www.miradormagazine.com/?page_id=1555.

"Driving & Community Mobility." AOTA, American Occupational Therapy Association, accessed December 2021, https://www.aota.org/practice/productive-aging/driving.aspx.

"Driving Safety and Alzheimer's Disease." Alzheimer's Caregiving, National Institute on Aging, accessed November 24, 2021, https://www.nia.nih.gov/health/driving-safety-and- alzheimers- disease#:~:text=When%20 a%20person%20with%20Alzheimer%27s%20disease%20is%20not,stop%20driving.%20Do%20this%20in%20a%20caring%20way.

"Education Center." Alzheimer's Association, accessed November 24, 2021. https://training.alz.org/?5=page/1/page-size/25.

"essentiALZ®—Alzheimer's Association Training and Certification." Alzheimer's Association, accessed November 24, 2021. https://www.alz.org/professionals/professional-providers/dementia-care-training- certification/essentialz-training-program-certification.

"For Teens." Alzheimer's Association, accessed November 23, 2021, https://www.alz.org/help- support/resources/kids-teens/for_teens.

"Getting Your Affairs in Order." National Institute on Aging, U.S. Department of Health and Human Services, last reviewed June 1, 2018, https://www.nia.nih.gov/health/getting- your-affairs-order.

Given, Carloyn and Max Wallack. *Why Did Grandma Put Her Underwear in the Refrigerator?* Scotts Valley, California: CreateSpace, 2013

"Grief and Loss as Alzheimer's Progresses." Alzheimer's Association, accessed November 29, 2021, https://www.alz.org/help-support/caregiving/caregiver-health/grief-loss-as- alzheimers-progresses.

Hammond, Scott D. "Caught In The Act: Inside An International Cartel." The United States Department of Justice, October 18, 2005, https://www.justice.gov/atr/speech/caught-act- inside-international-cartel.

"Helpline." Alzheimer's Association, accessed February 8, 2022. https://www.alz.org/help-support/resources/helpline.

"Help and Support." Alzheimer's Association, accessed November 24, 2021, https://www.alz.org/help-support.

"Home." Family Caregiver Alliance, accessed November 29, 2021, https://www.caregiver.org/

"Hospice Care." CaringInfo, National Hospice and Palliative Care Organization, accessed December 6, 2021, https://www.caringinfo.org/types-of-care/hospice-care/.

"How to talk about dementia with children and young people." Alzheimer's Society, accessed November 23, 2021, https://www.alzheimers.org.uk/get-support/daily-living/how-talk-dementia-children-young-people.

La Bey, Lori. Alzheimer's Speaks (*website*), accessed February 8, 2022, https://www.alzheimersspeaks.com/.

La Bey, Lori. *Alzheimer's Speaks Radio*, directed by Lori La Bey. 2011, San Antonio, Texas: BlogTalkRadio. Podcast. https://www.blogtalkradio.com/alzheimersspeaks

Langston, Laura. *Remember, Grandma?* New York City, New York: Viking Juvenile, 2004.

"Learn More About Safe Senior Driving." California Department of Aging, State of California, accessed December 29, 2021, https://aging.ca.gov/How_Do_I/Learn_More_About_Safe_Senior_Driving/.

Moreland, Jane P. "On Your Astonishment." *The Georgia Review*, Summer (1981). https://thegeorgiareview.com/authors/moreland-jane-p/.

Moreland, Jane P. "Prunings." *Poetry* 140, no. 3 (1982): 141-141. https://www.jstor.org/stable/20594532.

Oliveros, Jessie. *The Remember Balloons.* New York, New York: Simon & Schuster Books for Young Readers, 2018.

Shriver, Maria. *What's Happening to Grandpa?* New York City, New York: Little, Brown Books for Young Readers, 2004.

"Sleep Issues and Sundowning." Alzheimer's Association, accessed November 24, 2021, https://www.alz.org/help-support/caregiving/stages-behaviors/sleep-issues-sundowning.

"Suspicions and Delusions." Alzheimer's Association. Accessed November 23, 2021, https://www.alz.org/help-support/caregiving/stages-behaviors/suspicions-delusions.

Tauber, Beatrice, Psy.D. *Grandma and Me: A Kid's Guide for Alzheimer's and Dementia.* New York, New York: Morgan James Kids, 2017.

"Traveling." Alzheimer's Association, accessed November 24, 2021, https://www.alz.org/help- support/caregiving/safetytraveling.

Van Den Abelle, Veronique. *Still My Grandma.* Grand Rapids, Michigan: Eerdman's Books for Young Readers, 2007.

"What is Alzheimer's Disease?" Alzheimer's Association, accessed November 22, 2021, https://www.alz.org/alzheimers-dementia/what-is-alzheimers.

"What is Palliative Care?" CaringInfo, National Hospice and Palliative Care Organization, accessed December 6, 2021, https://www.caringinfo.org/types-of-care/palliative- care/#where.

About the Author

Mary Moreland is a lawyer living in Houston, Texas, and a single parent of two teenage sons. Together they share a dog, a cat, a turtle, and a fish. The bulk of Moreland's twenty-five-year legal career has been spent working on transactions outside the United States, principally in Latin America. In addition to her transactional work, Moreland has vast and deep knowledge of ethics and compliance matters, having served as chief compliance officer for two publicly traded international companies. *The Gap Between* is her first book.